MONTREAL OF YESTERDAY

מאָנטרעאל פון נעכטן

ווי דאָס אידישע לעבּען אין מאָנטרעאל
האָט זיך אַנטװיקעלט געזעלשאַפּטליך,
עקאָנאָמיש און קולטורעל אין די
לעצטע עטליכע צענדליג יאָהר

פון י. מדרש

„קענעדער אדלער" דרוקעריי   מאָנטרעאל—1947

PRINTED IN CANADA

[Title page, original Yiddish edition, 1947.]

Montreal of Yesterday

JEWISH LIFE IN MONTREAL, 1900-1920

Israel Medres

TRANSLATED FROM THE YIDDISH BY

Vivian Felsen

Véhicule Press

Véhicule Press acknowledges the on-going support of
The Canada Council for the Arts.

Cover design: J.W. Stewart; cover imaging: André Jacob
Cover photo of Russian-Jewish family is from the F. Goltman Collection,
Canadian Jewish Congress National Archives.
Cover photo of Bonsecours Market, 1915,
Archives of Ontario, C7-3-#1834.
Interior design and imaging: Simon Garamond
Printing: AGMV-Marquis Inc.

This translation is based on *Montreal fun Nekhtn*, Eagle Publishing Co., 1947,
with the permission of the Estate of Israel Medres
Copyright for translation, introduction, and notes © Vivian Felsen 2000
All rights reserved.
Dépôt légal, Bibliothèque nationale du Québec and the
National Library of Canada, third quarter 2000

CANADIAN CATALOGUING IN PUBLICATION DATA

Medres, Israel, 1894-1964
Montreal of yesterday

(Dossier Québec)
Translation of: Montreal fun nekhten, published
Montreal: Eagle Pub. Co., 1947.
ISBN: 1-55065-133-1

1. Jews–Quebec (Province)–Montréal–History–
20th century. 2. Jews–Quebec (Province)–Montréal–
Social conditions. 3. Jews–Quebec (Province)–Montréal–
Intellectual life. 4. Jews–Quebec (Province)–Montréal–
Politics and government. 1. Felsen, Vivian. 11. Title.
111. Series: Dossier Québec series.

FC2947.9.J4M4313 2000   971.4'28004924   C00-900312-6
F1054.5.M89J54 2000

Published by Véhicule Press, Montréal, Québec
www.vehiculepress.com

Distributed by General Distribution Services

Printed in Canada on alkaline paper.

To the children of
Israel and Sophie Medres

Sam and Anne
Abe and Barbara
Phil and Sylvia
Anne and Irvine Glass (my parents)

Israel Medres, *circa* 1930.

Contents

Preface to the Original Yiddish Edition 9

Translator's Preface 11

Introduction 13

The Jewish Neighbourhood 21

Immigrant Problems 24

Baron de Hirsch Institute 26

The Port of Montreal 31

Religious Observance 34

Sick Benefit Societies 40

At the *Arbeiter Ring* 45

Among the Poor 48

Class Divisions 50

The Extremists 52

The First Socialists 55

The First Jewish Bookstore 58

The Second Jewish Bookstore 61

Hebraists 64

Crisis 67

Mass Meetings 70

The *Keneder Adler* 73

Canada 76

The City 79

The Community 81

Writers 84

The Press 86

Boarders 89

The Monument National 92

Art and Business 97

The First Movies 100

Yiddish Vaudeville 102

Weddings 105
Zionist Dreamers 108
Zionist Politics 110
Zionist Radicals 112
The Historic Zionist Convention 115
Politics and Citizenship 118
Academic Anti-Semitism 121
The Attack on the Talmud 124
The Historic Decision 132
The Children's Strike Against Anti-Semitism 135
Yiddishism and Hebraism 137
Cloakmakers 139
Tailors 141
On the Eve of the Storm 143
The First World War 146
The War Years 149
Jewish Soldiers 152
Jewish Legionnaires 154
Relief Committees 156
Zionist War Policy 159
Real Estate 162
Transition 164
The Canadian Jewish Congress 166
Protest and Mourning 169
Festival of the Restoration 172
The New Immigrants 176
Immigrant Orphans 178
Farewell to Yesterday 179

TRANSLATOR'S NOTES 183
GLOSSARY 201
SELECTED BIBLIOGRAPHY 205
INDEX 209

Preface to the Original Yiddish Edition

Montreal of Yesterday by I. Medres takes the reader by the arm on a stroll through the streets of a world the reader has never truly left behind. Even if the reader no longer inhabits that world, Montreal of yesterday lives on in him. These memoirs of Jewish Montreal are a vital piece of the heritage of the reader and of the author, journalist and *felletonist* I. Medres—a man who stands at the frenzied wheel of the printing press spinning out, day after day, fresh damp pages of living history which fall like leaves, one atop the other, into heaps of valuable raw material lying in wait for historians of tomorrow.

Medres has roused these waiting leaves and momentarily opened for the reader a tiny window through which to view his past, reminding him that not long ago he was a very different person who bore the imprint of the old country, and had set out to acquire the stamp of a new world of which he has gradually become a part.

Although Medres narrates the events of yesterday in a very matter-of-fact way, as you read further you begin to sense that you are bidding farewell to a time which will never return. And that era is carrying away with it an entire world, a world of unique beauty and charm, of pioneering ideals, spiritual growth, openness to new ideas, and resounding hopes which were so very close to being realized. Although we, as immigrants, had landed in the very cauldron of American reality, there fluttered above us the wisp of a dream.

From today's perspective, which is so starkly realistic, indeed *naturalistic*, the reminiscences in I. Medres' book seem more fairy-tale than history. I suspect that the author of *Montreal of Yesterday* really wanted us to take a look at ourselves in the mirror of our past and become somewhat disoriented, not immediately recognizing ourselves. And perhaps I. Medres also had in mind to calm our present agitated, frantic, and feverish state with scenes and events of *Montreal of Yesterday*. In those days, on those streets, during those events, the pace was more relaxed. Jewish life was at the dawn of a new chapter in its history. There we can still distinguish the individual in the crowd; we hear his voice and watch him find his way.

I. Medres did not intend to write a history book, but simply to prepare materials for the use of future historians. He was the first to make some order of the strewn leaves, here and there adding a personal word or a picturesque description to throw a vivid light on the past.

J.I.Segal
1947

Translator's Preface

Shortly before her death in 1982, my mother, Anne Medres Glass, daughter of Israel Medres, had started translating the first few chapters of *Montreal of Yesterday* into English. A graduate of the Peretz School in Montreal and the Hekhere Kursn at the Shul far Yidish Vissen in New York (special courses designed for Yiddish teachers), she devoted much of her adult life to the teaching and promotion of Yiddish language and culture.

Then, in 1988, a paper on *Montreal of Yesterday* was presented at a conference on Yiddish in Montreal by Zachary Baker who at the time was Head of Technical Services at the Montreal Jewish Public Library. His paper was published in *An Everyday Miracle: Yiddish Culture in Montreal* (1990).

Finally, in 1997, *Montreal of Yesterday* appeared in French translation. Entitled *Le Montréal juif d'autrefois,* this book is one of several translations from the Yiddish by Pierre Anctil, former director of the Programme d'études canadiennes-françaises and research fellow in the Department of Jewish Studies, McGill University, and author of three books on the history of the Jews of Montreal. Pierre Anctil's scholarly translation, scrupulously faithful to the original Yiddish, provided the impetus for me to translate my grandfather's book into English.

In carrying out this project, I benefited from the contributions of a number of people. I am most indebted to both Pierre Anctil, currently Chercheur et réalisateur invité, Pointe-à-Callière, Musée d'archéologie et d'histoire de Montréal, and Zachary Baker, now Reinhard Family Curator of Judaica and Hebraica Collections, Stanford University Libraries, who provided me with their expertise and encouragement over the past two and a half years. I am extremely grateful to Chana Erlich of Toronto for sharing with me her exceptional linguistic capabilities.

In addition, I wish to thank Peter Heichelheim for his investigative skills; Roni Felsen for his technical assistance; Sylvia Lustgarten, former Director of the Committee for Yiddish of the Jewish Federation of Greater Toronto; Yuri Luryi, Professor Emeritus, University of Western Ontario; Janice Rosen, Director, Canadian Jewish Congress Archives; Bernard Katz,

Head, Special Collections and Library Development, University of Guelph; Joseph Glass, Halbert Centre for Canadian Studies at the Hebrew University of Jerusalem; Ralph Coram, Senior Archivist, Archives of Ontario; Christine Bourolias, Reference Archivist, Archives of Ontario; Nessa Olshansky-Ashtar; Ethel Raicus; and especially Simon Dardick of Véhicule Press. I am pleased to acknowledge the assistance of the Canada Council for the Arts in the form of a translation grant.

The enthusiastic participation of my husband and family, in particular my aunts and uncles, Abe and Barbara Madras, Philip and Sylvia Madras, made this project all the more meaningful. Unfortunately, my uncle Abe did not live to see it brought to completion.

Rummaging through the papers in my grandfather's desk,
April 1947, while he worked on *Montreal fun Nekhtn*.
Photo by Philip Madras.

Introduction

Montreal of Yesterday (Montreal fun Nekhtn) was originally published in Yiddish in 1947. It had earlier appeared in bi-weekly instalments[1] in the pages of the *Keneder Adler*[2] (the *Jewish Daily Eagle*), Montreal's Yiddish language newspaper. Israel Medres had been a staff writer for the newspaper for twenty-five years, contributing on a daily basis in numerous capacities including news editor, labour editor, court reporter, and publicist in the sense of political affairs columnist. His readers were the thousands of Yiddish-speaking Eastern European immigrants of Montreal who read the *Keneder Adler* not only for information about everything from world news to local events, but also for literary works of poetry, prose, and humour.

Medres was most admired and loved by his readers for his bi-weekly *felletons* which he wrote under the pen name Ben Mordecai. Unlike the French word "feuilleton" from which it derived, a *felleton* was a short personal essay on a public issue written in a light, almost humourous vein. Throughout his years as a staff writer for the *Keneder Adler*, Medres continued to pen these light-hearted short pieces on serious subjects which, like his other articles, were regularly reprinted in almost every Yiddish paper, including the United States and South America.

When reading *Montreal of Yesterday*, one should keep in mind that Medres was writing for his regular readers, many of whom had left Eastern Europe with no opportunity for a formal education but all of whom could read Yiddish and were eager for information about their newly adopted home and the world they had left behind. The genuine charm and gentle humour of his writing style is readily apparent, as is his ability to sketch a scene, a story, or an idea with a few carefully chosen words. The fifty-five short chapters of *Montreal of Yesterday*, each dealing with a different aspect of Jewish immigrant life in Montreal, are densely packed with facts and details, yet the reader absorbs them effortlessly. The language, which at first seems almost simplistic, in fact succeeds in conveying the richness and complexity of a period of rapid growth and colossal change.

When Medres wrote *Montreal of Yesterday*, in the aftermath of World

War II, the period from 1900 to 1920 already seemed remote. As J. I. Segal mentions in his preface to the original Yiddish edition, Montreal of yester-year seemed more figment than reality. The fervent hopes for a better world had been obliterated together with the thousands of Jewish towns and hamlets of Eastern Europe. By 1947, the immigration period had long ago come to an end and the future of world Jewry was uncertain. Canada had still not opened its doors to the remnants of European Jewry languishing in the D. P. camps.

In fact, more than a decade earlier, Medres had begun to muse on the uniqueness of the immigrant era, the years between 1900 and 1914 when immigration to Canada and the United States was virtually unrestricted and almost 30,000 Eastern European Jews had settled in Montreal alone.[3] In 1936, at the height of the Depression when the doors to immigration were already tightly shut, Medres wrote a series of articles for the *Canadian Jewish Chronicle*, the English-language publication of the Eagle Publishing Company, recalling with nostalgia the life of the newly-arrived immigrant Jews. Not only was Medres one of the earliest to recognize the significance of the immigrant era, even more remarkable is the fact that Medres was writing a true social history years before social history was considered a subject worthy of serious study in university history departments. While historians were continuing to focus their efforts on political and military events, Medres in 1936 was describing the places where people lived, the kind of jobs they had, how they courted and married, what books they read, what songs they sang, what plays they attended, what clothes they wore—all this and more in a language and writing style accessible to the immigrants themselves.[4]

In my research for this book and the life of Israel Medres, I have come across references to anglicisms in his Yiddish and indeed to anglicisms in the Yiddish of the *Keneder Adler*. As the prominent Yiddish poet Melech Ravitch noted,[5] Medres had an ear for the language of the Jewish masses. He was writing in the Yiddish used by the Jews of Montreal—in fact, by the Jews of North America. Moreover, such is the unique nature of the Yiddish language that it was open to the linguistic influences of the various host countries in which the Jews found themselves during their long exile.

Like Judeo-Arabic, Judeo-Persian and Judeo-Spanish (Ladino), to name but a few examples, Judeo-German, or Yiddish, evolved as Jews used the Hebrew alphabet in which they were literate to write the language in which they lived their daily lives. The Judeo-German spoken by the Jews who had migrated to the Rhineland around the year 1000, was eventually brought to Central and Eastern Europe as Jews fled the persecution engendered by the Crusades and the Black Death. Arriving in Poland from the twelfth century onward, the Jews of Ashkenaz, the Hebrew word for Germany, lived an autonomous yet circumscribed existence conducive to the perpetuation of their own language and culture. It was here in Poland, which in the sixteenth century became a vast kingdom encompassing Lithuania, Byelorussia (White Russia), and the Ukraine, that Yiddish flourished.

When Poland was partitioned between Austria, Prussia, and Russia in the late eighteenth century, the majority of Poland's Jews found themselves in Imperial Russia, but confined to the Pale of Settlement. Established to keep the Jews out of the rest of the Russian Empire, the Pale consisted of the fifteen *guberniias,* or provinces, east of Poland. It was from the Pale of Settlement, home to about eighty percent of Eastern European Jewry before World War I, that the majority of Montreal's Jews had immigrated. Almost every aspect of the lives of Montreal's Yiddish-speaking Jews was connected to people and events in Russia, where the Jews had maintained their separate and distinct identity while at the same time embracing the political ideas and ideologies of the modern world.

Jews in the Russian Empire suffered from the same lack of liberty as the rest of the population. However, over the years Jews had been subjected to an ever-increasing number of legal disabilities. They could neither settle upon, nor acquire, land outside cities and towns. Their attendance in secondary and higher schools of learning was severely restricted. Jews could neither vote nor run for office in the elections to local government institutions. They were prevented from becoming teachers or university professors.

By far the most serious restriction on the Jews, however, was their confinement to the Pale of Settlement where overcrowding and poverty made their existence intolerable. Only in exceptional cases could Jews reside elsewhere in the Empire. In many communities of the Pale, almost forty percent of the Jews were unemployed at the turn of the century, and almost as many depended on relief provided by Jewish welfare institutions.[6] Many artisans had begun to seek employment as industrial workers, especially in the textile and garment industries, in cities like Odessa, Vilna, and Bialystok. However, Jewish workers endured longer hours, lower wages, and more oppressive working conditions than their non-Jewish counterparts.[7]

In addition to the misery caused by legal disabilities, the Jews of Russia had to contend with the anti-Semitism of their Christian neighbours. Seen by Russians of every social class as enemies of the Orthodox Church, exploiters and corrupters of the peasantry, supporters of the revolutionary movement, and agents of foreign governments, the Jews could be used by the czarist regime as scapegoats in times of discontent. The pogroms of the 1880s sparked the first wave of emigration. In the late 1890s, with the spread of labour unrest, peasant disorders, student discontent, and demands for civil rights, reactionary elements in society began to appeal to the "national sentiments" of the masses. This led to the creation of new extreme right-wing anti-Semitic groups known as the Black Hundreds.[8]

According to the great Russian Jewish historian Simon Dubnow, the year 1897 was a turning point in the history of the Jews of Russia, for in that year a new national consciousness gave birth to two important Jewish political movements.[9] In 1897 the first Jewish political party was founded. Officially named the General Jewish Workers' Union of Russia, Poland, and Lithuania, it became known simply as the Bund. Although a socialist organization which stood for the brotherhood of the working classes, the Bund nevertheless encouraged Jewish nationalism. It provided lectures for workers in literature and history using Yiddish as the language of instruction and proclaiming it the national language of the Jews. The ideas and ideology of the Bund would also shape the Jewish community of Montreal, as Medres indicates in his book in the chapters on the *Arbeiter Ring*, the first socialists, the bookstores, and others. In 1897 the First Zionist Congress took place. Several chapters of the book show how Zionism, particularly Labour Zionism, played a leading role in the development of the Jewish community in Montreal.

At the same time, the Jewish intelligentsia in Russia, among them Dubnow, recognized the need to join the general struggle for liberation to ensure that Jews would be guaranteed their rights. As liberals, they shared the conviction that only in a constitutional democracy would the Jewish question be resolved. When, in October of 1905, Russia received its first constitution, they received the news with great joy.[10] Issued by Czar Nicholas II during the war with Japan, in which many Jews fought and died, and under threat of continued strikes and disorder throughout the Russian

Empire, the October Manifesto promised the freedoms of conscience, speech, assembly, and association, and provided for the convocation of a national parliament, the Duma, to be elected on the principle of universal suffrage. For the first time, the Jews of Imperial Russia had been granted the rights to vote and stand for election.

Since Jewish radicals, including the Bund, boycotted the elections hoping thereby to discredit the Duma and promote revolutionary aims, Jewish liberals were left to organize the election campaign in the Pale of Settlement. Young Jewish lawyers travelled throughout the Pale to explain the technicalities of voting to the Jewish masses, while local Jewish election committees helped Jewish voters to register.[11] These activities would be repeated in Montreal where the Citizenship League would be formed to encourage Jewish immigrants to exercise their franchise in municipal, provincial, and federal elections.

The Russian elections were held in the spring of 1906. The result was a Duma dominated by the liberal Constitutional Democratic Party, the Cadets. Its deliberations were closely followed by the Jews of Montreal for whom Miliukov and Maklakov, the Cadet leaders, were familiar names. When, within weeks, the Bialystok pogrom had left hundreds of Jews dead and wounded, among the non-Jewish Cadet deputies who made speeches in the Duma blaming the government for allowing and participating in the pogroms was Rodichev, whose speech was widely reported.[12] Russian Jews coming to Canada were more than pleased to discover by reading the *Keneder Adler* that Canada was governed by a Liberal government with cabinet ministers comparable to Miliukov, Maklakov, and Rodichev.[13]

The First State Duma was dissolved after only 73 days, in part for accusing the government of organizing pogroms. Thereafter, the Jews suffered more than ever as further restrictions were enacted and conditions in the Pale deteriorated. The failure of the First Duma meant the end of the participation of the Jewish intelligentsia in the liberation movement, and the recognition that the only alternatives left to the Jews of Russia were revolution or emigration.

Medres in his book reveals the impact of these events on the Jews of Montreal. Among the Montreal Jewish socialists and members of the *Arbeiter Ring* were those who had manned the barricades during the 1905 revolution, who had spent time in czarist prisons or in Siberia, and who continued to talk and act as though they were still living in czarist Russia. Medres even records the Russian songs they were still singing in Montreal. He notes that more educated Jews arrived in Montreal after the 1905 revolution and the failure of the Duma, becoming the first teachers in the Jewish schools, community activists, and writers for the *Keneder Adler*, founded in 1907.

The Poalei Zion, the Labour Zionist party, was outlawed in Russia in 1906, its membership dropping from 25,000 in 1905 to 300 due to arrests, exile, or emigration.[14] The Labour Zionists then became very active in the United States and Canada where they founded the national radical schools and the movement for the establishment of a Jewish Congress, and initiated the drive for volunteers to the Jewish Legion battalions led by Yitzhak Ben-Zvi and David Ben-Gurion, all of which Medres describes in his book.

Israel Jonah Medres, born in 1894 in the Pale in the small town of Liachovici[15] in Byelorussia, was only a child during what Dubnow has termed the terrible years from 1903 to 1906, years of pogroms, war with Japan, a failed revolution, and a failed constitution. In 1907, at the age of thirteen, after attending the traditional *kheder*, Jewish school for boys, he went to study in the Lida Yeshiva, also in Byelorussia which was part of the geographic entity the Jews referred to as Lithuania, *Lite* in Yiddish. Jewish Lithuania, under the influence of the Vilna Gaon, had for the most part rejected the mysticism of Hasidism in favour of a more rational approach to religion, and was receptive to the Haskalah, the Jewish Enlightenment, which advocated an openness to scientific progress and European scholarship. This attitude was particularly evident at the Lida Yeshiva established by Rabbi Jacob Reines (1839-1915) who brought modern methodology to the teaching of religious subjects and introduced secular studies into the curriculum.[16]

In the Lida Yeshiva, Medres was also exposed to the Zionist ideas of Rabbi Reines, one of the first rabbis to join Theodore Herzl in the face of opposition from most of the rabbis of Europe. In 1902 Rabbi Reines founded the Mizrahi movement, the first religious Zionist organization, which soon had hundreds of branches throughout the Pale of Settlement, Rumania, Austria-Hungary, Germany, Switzerland, and North America.[17] Medres spent three years in the Lida Yeshiva, his only formal education, but one that would prepare him for his vocation as a Yiddish journalist and lead to his future close association with the Labour Zionists in Montreal.

Of the more than two million Jews who left the Pale of Settlement between 1880 and 1917, most emigrated to the United States. With an uncle already settled in Nova Scotia, Medres in 1910, and at the age of

sixteen, set out for Canada. His boat docked in Montreal, and here he remained. At first he worked at various menial jobs before going to work in
a tailor shop. In 1914 he married Sophie Wigdor (Victor),[18] originally from
the tiny town of Leckava (*Latskeve* in Yiddish), in Lithuania near the Latvian
border. As a teenager, she had come alone to Canada and worked in a garment
factory, saving enough to send steamship tickets to her parents and three
younger siblings, all of whom settled in Montreal. On the other hand,
Israel Medres never saw his parents or siblings again, except for a younger
sister, a baby when he left Europe, who made contact with him in the
1950s after reading one of his articles in a Buenos Aires Yiddish newspaper.
Travelling to meet her in Argentina for the first time in 1960, he wrote a
series of articles for the *Keneder Adler* about the Jews of Mexico and Argentina.[19]

After writing the occasional *felleton* for the *Keneder Adler*, in 1922 Medres
became a full-time staff writer. Until his death in 1964, for over forty
years, hardly an issue of the newspaper appeared without an article by
Medres. He was also the Montreal correspondent for the New York
newspaper *Morgn Zhurnal*, and edited *Dos Vort*, the official organ of the
Montreal Labour Zionists. *Montreal of Yesterday* is one of two books Israel
Medres wrote. The second, *Between Two World Wars* (*Tsvishn Tsvey Velt Milkhomes*),
was published just before his death.

After his death Medres' work continued to be quoted, reprinted, and
translated. In the Canadian Jewish Archives Series on the history of the
Jews in Canada published between 1974 and 1996, historian David Rome
relied heavily on articles by Medres. Biographies of Medres are included in
the major lexicons of Yiddish writers, and his name appears in histories of
Yiddish literature as well as books about the Jews of Canada.

The wealth of material my grandfather left behind in the form of articles
and *felletons* and their significance for future historians was noted early on
by his contemporaries, writers such as J.I.Segal, Melekh Ravitch,[20] and
Joseph Gallay.[21] Yet the bulk of his work, and in particular his two books,
could be read only by an increasingly limited number of Yiddish readers.

In 1997 Pierre Anctil's French translation of *Montreal fun Nekhtn* was
published.[22] The first to recognize the importance of Medres' book for the
study of Quebec history, Pierre Anctil has made it accessible to francophone
students[23] and historians who have since cited Medres in their work.[24] In
addition to their historic value, those passages of *Montreal of Yesterday* dealing
with French-Jewish relations in Quebec exemplify Medres' journalistic

even-handedness, much lauded by his peers.[25]

I am delighted to now introduce *Montreal of Yesterday* to an even wider audience, including those with roots in Jewish Montreal at the dawn of the twentieth century.

The old neighbourhood.
Guide de Montréal,
XXIe Congrès eucharistique internationale, 1910.

The Jewish Neighbourhood

THE LAST FEW DECADES have witnessed tremendous changes in Montreal. The appearance of the city has been almost totally transformed since the turn of the century when Montreal resembled a small town. Neighbourhoods once considered "out of town" are today traversed by spacious streets and graceful boulevards lined with modern apartment buildings, large factories, and department stores. Montreal has become one of the most important cities on the North American continent.

During this same period social, economic, and cultural changes have profoundly affected the life of the Jewish population, both materially and spiritually. At the turn of the century, Montreal already had a vibrant Jewish community, but with little resemblance to the one of today. There were other problems and other attitudes toward Jewish life and life in general. The approach to community affairs was different, as were tastes in culture, literature, and theatre. It was a happier time when people did not know the meaning of world wars, concentration camps, or gas chambers. The Jews of that time could never have imagined a First World War, the rise of Hitler, and a Second World War which would annihilate a major part of the Jewish people and eradicate centuries of traditional Jewish life in Europe.

To become acquainted with the life of the Jewish immigrants in the not too distant past, with their problems, their aspirations, their ambitions, we must revisit the old Jewish neighbourhood and take a stroll through Montreal of yesterday.

A tour of the Jewish neighbourhood as it existed forty years ago[1] will take us downtown into narrow streets and lanes where very few Jews can be seen today. Let us turn into Dorchester Street[2] which forty years ago was throbbing with Jewish life. The corner of St. Urbain and Dorchester was the very heart of the Jewish neighbourhood. Nearby was Dufferin Park, then a "Jewish park" where Jewish immigrants went to breathe the fresh air, meet their *landslayt*,[3] hear the latest news, look for work, and read the newspapers.

Close by was Dufferin School, where Jewish immigrant children distinguished themselves with the highest grades. Many prominent Jews today will recall that they studied at that school.

In the same neighbourhood, on St. Urbain near La Gauchetière, was the Talmud Torah, the first important Jewish educational institution built by immigrant Jews and, for a long time, the only such institution. Forty years ago there were hardly any Jewish children in Montreal. Many Jews had left their wives and children in Europe. Here in Montreal they lived alone as boarders, saving their dollars to purchase steamship tickets to bring their families across the ocean.

Continuing our walk, we approach Craig Street[4] where all the side streets and lanes such as St. Urbain, Clark (then St. Charles-Borromée), St. George,[5] Coté,[6] Hermine, St. Dominique, and Cadieux,[7] were inhabited exclusively by Jews. Jews also lived on the other side of Craig Street— along Notre Dame Street, St. Maurice Street, and Dupré Lane near Hay-market.[8] Today almost no Jews remain in this part of town.[9]

The Jewish neighbourhood also extended "uptown." "Uptown" meant the area between Dorchester and Ontario and around Duluth Street. The more affluent Jews lived on Prince Arthur, Ontario, and other streets nearby, and a small group of the wealthiest Jews lived on Sherbrooke Street, near University and McGill College Avenue.

Several important synagogues were located in the very heart of the Jewish neighbourhood. There was the Rumanian Shul (Beth David) on Chénéville Street near Dufferin Park. On St. Urbain Street, near St. Catherine, stood the Chevra Kadisha Shul, on Cadieux, near Vitré,[10] the Russian Shul (B'nai Jacob), and on La Gauchetière, near Coté, the Chevra Shaas Shul. One of the few synagogues from that time still in existence is the Austrian Shul on Milton Street.

In those days Jewish workers were employed in the tailoring and cloakmaking shops which were located for the most part around Notre Dame and St. Paul Streets. The more established Jews owned stores on Notre Dame Street,[11] Craig Street and Main Street,[12] between Craig and Sherbrooke. The storekeepers were the first to acculturate because they had to deal on a daily basis with non-Jewish customers and therefore were compelled to learn the language of the land as quickly as possible.

Every Saturday afternoon the inhabitants of the Jewish neighbourhood could be seen making their way to Dufferin Park. There they would meet their *landslayt*, talk about the old country and about their new home. Those immigrants who were already more or less established would offer advice and suggestions to the immigrants who were still entirely "green." The advice concerned finding a job, adapting generally to the new environment, and learning the manners and customs of the new homeland as quickly as possible.

Prince Arthur and Cadieux streets.
(Cadieux became de Bullion in 1927.)
Notman Photographic Archives.

Immigrant Problems

THE MOST PRESSING PROBLEM facing the newly arrived immigrant was to find a job that would allow him to earn a living and advance economically. If an individual was sponsored by a relative who was already established, his greatest problem was solved. The relative would assist the immigrant in finding employment or, if self-employed, take him into the business.

There were many immigrants, however, whose families could not assist them and some who had no relatives here at all. Such immigrants would consult their more established *landslayt* who were quite forthcoming in their advice. Often the *landslayt* counselled the newcomer to work in a clothing factory, starting out as a presser or a lining maker to learn the trade.

Tailoring in the old country, they had to admit, was a lowly trade, but in America it was an honour to be a tailor. Many decent and respectable European Jews who came to Canada took up this trade. They would also point to prominent clothing manufacturers, distinguished members of the Baron de Hirsch Institute as well as of the opulent Shaar Hashomayim Synagogue, who had started out as simple tailors.

On the other hand, there were *landslayt* who would strongly discourage anyone from going to work in a clothing factory. Tailoring in America, they argued, meant a meagre existence, plagued by endless layoffs and strikes. A tailor would forever remain a pauper. And, they warned, working too long in a clothing factory one was sure to contract hemorrhoids or—heaven forbid!—consumption.

Some *landslayt* advised becoming a *klapper*[13] for a custom-peddler. They reasoned as follows: "From a *klapper* you can work your way up to become a custom-peddler.[14] After that, if you are clever, you can become the proprietor of a dry goods store on Main Street or on Notre Dame Street. Eventually you could end up a wholesaler." And the *landslayt* would name several distinguished residents of Montreal, prominent merchants or wholesalers, who had started out as *klappers,* selling door to door. . . .

Alternatively, *landslayt* would advise becoming a country peddler.

Admittedly the life of a country peddler was not easy, but his work led to more rapid acculturation and financial success. After working in the country for only a few months, a shrewd peddler would be able to settle down in a small town, open a store, buy a house and earn a comfortable living. On Rosh Hashana and Yom Kippur, he could come to the city, buy a seat in a synagogue, and be "all right!"

Immigrant Jews were also advised to work for the CPR in the railway yards on Davidson Street near Rachel. At that time the CPR employed many Jews as locksmiths, carpenters, and tinsmiths. They were even hired without any knowledge of the national languages. The foremen would stipulate wages and assign work entirely in sign language.

Factory worker Faige Fremder, 17, in 1917.
She died in the flu epidemic of 1918.
Archives of Ontario AO 4776 / F1405-23-103 / MSR 8427 #1

The Baron de Hirsch Institute

AT THE BEGINNING of this century, the Baron de Hirsch Institute was the hub of Jewish philanthropic and social activity. At first immigrants would be under the impression that the imposing building bearing the name Baron de Hirsch Institute actually belonged to the Baron. They had been familiar with the name of Baron de Hirsch[15] in the old country where they had heard a great deal about him. Thus they believed that as a rich Jew he owned houses in several cities, including Montreal. But before long the immigrants discovered that in fact the house belonged not to the Baron de Hirsch but to Montreal Jewry as a whole.

The more established *landslayt* would tell the newer immigrants the following story about the Baron de Hirsch Institute. A small group of Montreal Jews, having read in the newspaper that Baron de Hirsch helped to settle impoverished Jews on agricultural land, wrote him a letter requesting that he turn his attention to Canada. They informed him that the Canadian Jewish community was rapidly expanding thanks to a continuous flow of immigrants from Eastern Europe, many of whom could be settled on farms. The Baron did indeed take an interest in Canada, and in his reply to the letter, enclosed a large cheque. Hence his name was immortalized on the building[16] which became the centre of Jewish communal activity in Montreal.

From today's perspective, Jewish community activity in those years was rather limited. The Baron de Hirsch Institute was responsible for the care of the needy. Although upon their arrival newcomers were under the impression that poor Jews were only to be found in the old country, they were soon to discover that there were widows, orphans, and the chronically unemployable among the immigrants. Abandoned wives required support while their missing husbands, who had fled to other cities, were being tracked down. Some Jews fell ill after arriving here and required assistance.

An immigrant frequenting the Baron de Hirsch Institute on a Sunday afternoon or evening would encounter the already established members of the community attending meetings. In many of the meeting rooms only

English was spoken. If the immigrant did not yet understand English, friends and *landslayt* would urge him to enroll in the English classes offered in the evenings by the Institute.

Thirty or forty years ago, the night school at the Baron de Hirsch Institute was one of the most important institutions for Jewish immigrants. In the night school newcomers zealously applied themselves to the study of English. The younger men who saw the language as their key to success, had another reason for attending night school. There they could meet immigrant girls who were also learning English. Classroom encounters blossomed into romances, romances into marriages.

Not all newly arrived immigrants could attend night school. Middle-aged people working hard to make a living and lacking an aptitude for learning did not enroll, or else they would sign up only to drop out soon afterward. Instead, these people made an effort to learn English on the street, from their neighbours or co-workers. The first English words they would learn were "hurry up," "come on," "time is money," "help yourself," "never mind," and "what do you want." A Jewish immigrant factory worker would hear the phrase "hurry up" at every turn. The foreman as well as his co-workers would impress upon him that on this side of the ocean everything had to be done quickly, in a hurry. By working fast you work your way up and become "all right." Another related expression was "time is money." *Landslayt* and friends would explain that time spent not working was money lost.

Thus the Jewish immigrants did their utmost to work faster to avoid the foreman's wrath. If this hurried pace was difficult to bear, they poured out their bitter hearts against Christopher Columbus. In those days disgruntled immigrants would often decry Columbus.

Many hoped that as soon as they had mastered the English language, they would leave the factory with its foreman and "hurry ups," and buy a small business of their own. In fact, a large number of these discontented factory workers who had learned English on the street were able to do just that. Later they expanded their businesses and today their children are well-to-do citizens and prominent businessmen who play an important role in the city's Jewish community.

Younger immigrants quickly adapted to the new ways in their new country thanks to the night school in the Baron de Hirsch. By attending English classes several times a week, they began to feel at home there. They looked around, met new people, and became aware of the various social events taking place in the city. They discovered that they could participate in certain activities while they were still green, even before they could speak English.

Once he felt at home at the Baron de Hirsch Institute, the immigrant began to meet members of the Jewish intelligentsia—*maskilim* from the old country who spoke fluent Hebrew, Hebrew teachers, Jews who wrote for the *Keneder Adler*, Jews involved in Zionist organizations or radical groups. They spoke to him in a friendly manner and urged him to stop pining for the old country despite the back-breaking work in the factory where the foreman was always admonishing him to "hurry up," where freedom and independence were non-existent. They would say to him, "Learn English, and everything will be all right. All of America will be open to you. You can become a salesclerk in a store, a news agent on the trains or a sewing machine salesman. Thank heaven that you are free of Russian thieves and Rumanian rascals. Learn English."

Thus they spoke to the immigrant Jews coming to learn English at the Baron de Hirsch night school. The immigrants studied assiduously with profound respect for the teachers. Mr. Gordon, who was then the principal of the night school, was highly regarded by the immigrants who were grateful to him for teaching them the language of the country.

Several bright young immigrants were gifted students and turned their knowledge to good advantage. Proficiency in English enabled them to escape the tailor shops and cloak shops and enter occupations where they were quickly Canadianized, facilitating their climb to success. Many became clerks and salesmen in stores and wholesale establishments and soon the foreignness disappeared from their faces and clothing. Others who started out as sewing machine salesmen ended up as insurance agents. Still others worked on trains as news agents.

Indeed, the news agent on the train was often the first Jew in Canada the immigrants would encounter after leaving the ship at Quebec or Halifax. Never would it have occurred to them that the man in uniform selling newspapers and snacks was one of their own, a Jew. But when the news agent began to speak to them in Yiddish, they immediately knew that he was a Jew from the old country. They discovered that not so long ago he too was a newcomer on the train from Quebec or Halifax. The news agent was the first to welcome them and inform them that they were coming to a land of work. All must work, but if one works, one is paid and is "all right."

Immigrants coming to the Baron de Hirsch Institute to learn English also discovered a library, the first they had seen in Montreal. Those among them who had read books in the old country were elated and took great pleasure in visiting the library to read or watch others read. There they found many books and journals in English. The ordinary immigrant who frequented the library longed to be able to read these books and journals as soon as possible. Then he would no longer be green.

Meanwhile, he admired those Jews who could already read English. They seemed so very different from the people he met on the street or in the factory—more intelligent, friendlier. The people he met at the library discussed culture, books, magazines, and newspapers. They would tell him that there were Jews in Canada who devoted their time to writing books on various subjects—history, poetry, and current events. They would assure him that those who applied themselves to reading and self-education were not missing out on opportunities for advancement. On the contrary, they were at an advantage.

They would counsel him as to which meetings to attend to make the right friends, friends who thought and felt as he did. He was encouraged to believe that before long he too would master English and be able to read the important books in the library such as those by Zangwill[17] who was then the most popular writer among Jews who could speak and read English.

From the intellectuals at the Baron de Hirsch, the immigrant heard a great deal about Harris Vineberg, a short man with a small beard who was a clothing manufacturer. Vineberg was said to be the man who had written the letters to the Baron de Hirsch resulting in the Baron's financial support for Jewish colonization in Canada. At that time there was much discussion and activity with regard to the settlement of Jewish immigrants on farms. The immigrant intellectuals who frequented the Baron de Hirsch library had a profound respect for this work and therefore admired Harris Vineberg for having written letters to the Baron, to the Alliance Israelite, and to prominent Jews in London and Paris.[18]

On the street, however, among the immigrant workers who did not attend the Baron de Hirsch Institute, Harris Vineberg was known only as a clothing manufacturer, and clothing manufacturers at that time personified capitalist exploitation. They were far from popular. It was known that in

Vineberg's shop the workers, all of them Jewish, worked long hours while the union waged a constant battle against him.

The intellectual immigrants always sympathized with the discontented workers in their struggle against the manufacturers. However, when they came to the Baron de Hirsch, they greatly respected the wealthy Jews who devoted themselves to colonization, helping newly arrived Jewish immigrants from Russia and Rumania to settle on farms and become productive and useful citizens.

One of the important leaders of the community at that time was David Ansell.[19] Ansell was a British Jew who, as Consul General for Mexico, had more dealings with Mexicans than with Jews. He was, however, not only a diplomat and businessman, but also an author who wrote about the foreign policy of England. He was a director of the Baron de Hirsch Institute and very active in the colonization project.

Another outstanding Jewish leader was also a consul for a foreign government. Clarence de Sola,[20] of whom more will be said later, was well-known among the intellectuals for being the president of the Zionist Organization and the brother of a rabbi.

The immigrants at the Baron de Hirsch Institute would also hear a great deal about Lazarus Cohen,[21] father of Lyon Cohen.[22] Lazarus Cohen was known to all the immigrant Jews, even those who never visited the Institute, for four reasons. He was one of the founders of the Talmud Torah, he was the brother of Rabbi Zvi Cohen,[23] he had a long, patriarchal beard, and he owned a metal factory which employed many immigrant Jewish workers. Lazarus Cohen and his son Lyon Cohen were among the leading personalities in the Baron de Hirsch Institute.

The immigrants were also told about Abraham Kaplansky,[24] a Jew from Bialystok who later became the Superintendent of the Institute. Although Kaplansky was not one of the more affluent Jews, he travelled in their circles. He was one of those community leaders who tried to forge links between the immigrant Jews from Eastern Europe and the already established Jews who had come to Canada decades earlier.

It was said of Kaplansky that he was the first to introduce Hebrew typography to Montreal for the printing of leaflets and circulars. Before Kaplansky opened his Montreal printing shop, all Yiddish leaflets had to be printed in New York. For a time the Yiddish leaflet was the only means of communicating with the Jewish population of Montreal.

The Port of Montreal

THE PORT OF MONTREAL is known as one of the busiest in North America. From the Montreal harbour ships sail to all four corners of the globe, many laden with wheat and other Canadian products. The streets near the harbour are the oldest in the city. The earliest buildings are located on and around de la Commune and St. Paul streets.

Nowadays people living in the Jewish neighbourhood see little of the harbour. Few occasions arise for visiting the waterfront, nor is there much interest. The ships that cross the Atlantic are no longer familiar; they no longer bring friends and *landslayt* from the old country. The names of ships once known to all the immigrants have been long forgotten.

In the old days, however, when the Jewish neighbourhood was near Craig Street, the Jewish immigrant had many opportunities to visit the port and its environs. Immigrant Jews went there in search of employment. At that time there were Jewish longshoremen loading and unloading the ships. For this type of work one had to be in excellent physical condition. Among the immigrant Jews there were many strapping young men with ruddy cheeks and broad shoulders who in the old country had been engaged as blacksmiths and porters or at other types of heavy labour. Some had left Russia solely to avoid serving in the czarist army. The numbers fleeing military service peaked during the time of the Russo-Japanese war and the unsuccessful revolution against the Czar in 1905 and 1906.

Many of these robust young men earned a good living at the docks. They quickly became Canadianized because of their daily contact with non-Jews. An immigrant who worked at the docks was treated with special respect and a girl who became betrothed to such a young man received the hearty congratulations of her friends and *landslayt*. They would say that she had entered the new country "on the right foot."

Montreal Jews also visited the harbour because of St. Helen's Island. Every Sunday Jewish families would go to St. Helen's Island to enjoy the fresh air and greenery. The trip to the island was interesting. The boat was much smaller, of course, than those which transported Jewish immigrants across the Atlantic. Nevertheless it was a boat with a captain, life belts, and all the other ship's accessories. The cost of the trip was a modest five cents, and one paid only for the ride to the island. The return trip was free.

For immigrant Jews this island was a paradise where they felt very much at ease. They would meet people who had come from the same town or hamlet in the old country, some of whom were newcomers, others partly established and many already well established.

It was very easy to recognize those who were well established. Many of them could be identified because they appeared well dressed and contented. One could see that they were financially successful. They sported watches with gold chains over their vests, massive gold rings on their fingers, and gold teeth. Of such a person it was said, "He's been in the country for a long time and he's already—*keneynehore* (may the evil eye be averted)—all right!"

Others could be recognized because they looked thin and haggard, with sunken eyes. Their clothing, although strictly American, was very worn. If one were to speak to such an "established" person, he would say, "Yes, I have been here in this golden land for a long time. I have been through layoffs and strikes and recessions. Enough to darken my days . . ."

When *landslayt* and friends met on St. Helen's Island they would discuss problems in the community, troubles of their own, and sometimes even world issues. Community problems usually arose from disputes with the bakers and butchers who wanted to raise the prices of bread and meat. Only the more enlightened immigrants who read the newspapers on a daily basis would discuss world affairs. The majority of immigrants had no time to read newspaper articles about politics. They would read only the lighter pieces.

Therefore most talked about themselves and their own difficulties. The most common topic of conversation was the adjustment to the new country. Many immigrants were discontented, and, cursing Christopher Columbus, they would long for the old country where life seemed more peaceful and they had been free—free of the factory and the foreman.

Others, who were happy, would bless Columbus and curse Czar Nicholas saying, "The land of Columbus is a golden land. When your work is done, you are a free man, free as a bird. You may go where you please, mind your own business . . . no foreman . . . no boss . . . you can do what you want with your *payday*. . . ."[25]

To this the discontented immigrant would retort, "The worker is like a slave . . . he lives in constant fear . . . he is at the mercy of the foreman . . . he is not free." And he would add, "Man is alone . . . no friends . . . every man for himself . . . help yourself . . ."

But the contented immigrants would counter, "The worker is free. He need fear no one, a policeman cannot harm him. It is not like under Czar Nicholas. Here there is no compulsory military service. A son with a good head on his shoulders can go to college . . ."

Many of the contented immigrants had sons with good heads on their shoulders going to college and graduating as lawyers and doctors. They are now among Montreal's Jewish professionals.

Advertisement in 1910-1911 almanac.
Dubitsky Collection,
Canadian Jewish Congress National Archives.

Religious Observance

THE BAGGAGE of the immigrant Jews arriving in the early years of this century had little room for religion. The proportion of truly traditional Jews was then much higher than it is today. But even the religious Jews had left much of their religious observance behind.

Very few Jews were interested in Jewish education. Most were convinced that teaching religious observance to children born in Canada was a wasted effort. To the typical orthodox Jew at that time, Jewish education in essence meant learning to recite the *kaddish* and preparing for Bar Mitzvah. For this purpose, in addition to the Talmud Torah, there were special private teachers, *melamdim*, whom the immigrant Jews called "peddlers of Judaism".

The religious immigrant arrived in Canada resigned to the idea that neither a foundation nor a future existed for traditional Judaism. Therefore he was concerned with only two things: first, to have kosher meat in his home, and secondly, to have his son be able to say *kaddish* after him when the time came. He had given up any hope of maintaining other Jewish religious practices. He saw too many Jews, including orthodox Jews, working on the Sabbath, and he was also aware that in radical circles a vigorous campaign was being conducted against religion. He lived with the frightening thought that he belonged to the last generation of orthodox Jews in America. In later years, when more rabbis and scholars arrived from Europe, the religious immigrants became better organized and their pessimistic attitude disappeared.

The whole matter of the Bar Mitzvah seemed very strange to the immigrant Jews who came from the religious environment of the small towns of Russia, Poland, Rumania, and Galicia. They were amazed upon entering the synagogue on a Saturday morning to witness a Bar Mitzvah ceremony. They were most impressed to see a small, Canadian-born boy with a *talles* over his shoulders take his place on the podium, chant the prayers and *Haftarah* with a strange intonation, and even deliver a sermon. In the old country they had never seen such a ceremony.

At first, the religious Jew found the Bar Mitzvah ceremony unpleasant to watch. Of course he enjoyed seeing a young boy who was born in Canada come to the synagogue, wear a prayer shawl, and sing the blessings before and after the Torah reading. At the same time, however, he was critical. To him, this was not authentic Jewish observance but something mechanical and artificial. All too often the immigrant Jew saw the Bar Mitzvah boy surrounded only by women—his mother, an aunt, another aunt. When he inquired after the father, he was told that the father was busy at work, and the uncles as well. The real Bar Mitzvah party would take place the following day, Sunday, when the father and uncles would be off work.[26]

As I have mentioned, immigrant Jews did not expect any more from a Jewish education beyond the *kaddish* and Bar Mitzvah speeches. It was their conviction that the one and only home for Judaism was the old country. If there were a need for rabbis, ritual slaughterers, sextons, or cantors— they could be imported from Europe. Jewish immigrants in those days could never have imagined that some day there would be yeshivas in Montreal, that Canadian-born young men would go to study in American seminaries and graduate as rabbis, or that their Canadian-born sons and daughters would drive their children to large, modern Talmud Torahs, where Jewish studies would be taught on the highest level.

Religious Jews coming to Montreal were confronted by a host of difficulties, but the main problem was Sabbath observance. Orthodox Jews were very anxious to find jobs that did not require them to work on Saturdays. They could not work for the CPR where Jewish workers were welcome. Nor could they work at the docks. They had to find places of employment which were closed on Saturdays.

On the other hand, they could go to work in clothing shops, most of which closed on Saturdays. Many orthodox Jews with long, patriarchal beards were employed by H. Vineberg, Kellert, and Levinson. Although the bearded orthodox Jews who worked in the clothing shops were politically far from radical, they became active members of the garment workers' union and loyal adherents of the principle of worker solidarity. Many of these immigrants became tailors for one reason only: they were unable to find another occupation which did not require work on the Sabbath.

However, many immigrants were not suited for the needle trades. At that time the contractors and foremen were very particular when they went to Dufferin Park to find immigrants to work as tailors. They would examine the immigrant carefully, especially his fingers. If the immigrant's hands and fingers appeared clumsy, he was not a good prospect but perhaps he could be a presser. Not every immigrant was willing to be a presser.

When an orthodox immigrant did not qualify as a needle worker he was compelled to seek work elsewhere, and then the problem of Sabbath observance became acute. Sometimes he would search relentlessly and find no job that would leave his Saturdays free. His *landsdlayt* and friends would gather to offer advice. Some friends advised him to decide once and for all to work on Saturdays and be done with the problem. Others counselled him to open a small business that required no capital or experience such as becoming a peddler. Then he could rest on the Sabbath.

A substantial number of religious immigrants followed this advice and became self-employed. They began with small businesses which expanded over time. Many of them now own large companies and they, or their children, are among the leading businessmen in the city.

Upon arriving in Montreal, the immigrant was assured by friends and townsmen that he would find no shortage of synagogues in the city. And true enough, on an ordinary Saturday, the immigrant was welcome in any synagogue he entered.

If he wished, he could go to the uptown synagogues where the more prosperous Jews attended services. The uptown synagogues were the German Shul (Shaar Hashomayim) on McGill College Avenue and the Spanish-Portuguese Synagogue (Shearith Israel) on Stanley Street. The wealthier Jews also frequented the Temple Emanu-El. However, in that era, Jewish immigrants had no interest in the Temple. A wide chasm separated the orthodox from the Reform Jews.

During that period orthodox rabbis and nationalist writers sharply attacked the Reform movement as assimilationist and anti-nationalist. Even Rabbi Stephen Wise,[27] although he was an active Zionist, came under attack because he was a pillar of the Reform movement in America. The majority of Reform rabbis were passionately anti-Zionist. Only in later years, in the wake of tremendous changes, did Zionism make significant inroads in the Reform movement. Most American rabbis today are Zionists. The Temple Emanu-El in present-day Montreal is a centre of Jewish communal activity and its rabbi, Dr. H. Stern,[28] is an active Zionist. But during the immigrant period, there was absolutely no social interaction between orthodox Jews and Temple members.

However, an orthodox Jew would certainly visit the German Synagogue on McGill College Avenue. As soon as he entered, he would notice that many of the worshippers were well-to-do but few were German. Most of the congregants were Eastern European. Even the rabbi, Dr. H. Abramowitz,[29] was not a German Jew.

Similarly, in the Spanish and Portuguese Synagogue, the immigrant would find more East European Jews than Spanish Jews. While the Spanish Synagogue differed greatly in appearance from the synagogues which the immigrant had known in Europe, the German shul was similar to the more opulent synagogues he would have seen in the larger cities and towns of Russia and Rumania.

Landslayt would explain that the Spanish and Portuguese Jews had never actually set foot in Spain or Portugal, nor did they speak Spanish or Portuguese. They were the descendants of Jews who had lived in Spain and Portugal hundreds of years ago and from there had migrated to Holland, Belgium or England. Subsequently their offspring, who immigrated to Canada about 150 years ago, founded the first Jewish congregation and the first synagogue.

For a long time, the Spanish Jews were the only Jews in Montreal. Then, at the beginning of the 19th century, German Jews began to arrive, forced to flee by the political unrest in Germany, Austria, and Hungary, where many Jews had taken part in the struggles against despots and reactionaries. Upon arriving here, the German Jews became involved in the import-export business and built factories. At first they attended services at the Spanish and Portuguese Synagogue on St. James Street, and later on Chénéville Street.

Eventually, however, the Spanish Synagogue became too crowded. So about one hundred years ago, the German Jews who were unaccustomed to the Sephardic ritual founded the Shaar Hashomayim Congregation. At first the members of this congregation assembled in a private home on St. Gabriel Street, near the harbour, then the centre of town. Later they decided to build a synagogue on Cadieux Street near Vitré. At the time it was a fashionable neighbourhood and their building was beautiful by contemporary standards. Later the wealthier members of the congregation began to move further uptown into the "aristocratic" part of town situated between

University and Guy Streets, and conceived the idea of building a new synagogue uptown. The synagogue they constructed on McGill College Avenue was known as the German Synagogue. The old building on Cadieux was taken over by the newly founded B'nai Jacob Congregation and came to be known as the Russian shul.

Thus the *landslayt* explained to the newcomers about the uptown synagogues, the German and the Spanish and Portuguese Synagogues. And if the immigrant were to ask why it is that nowadays so few German Jews are found in the German shul and so few Spanish Jews in the Spanish and Portuguese Synagogue, informed *landslayt* would answer that the majority of German and Spanish Jews had assimilated into the non-Jewish population. Their integration was an easy and natural process because, apart from the synagogue, they had founded no Jewish institutions for their children. The young people were raised in a Christian environment and married Christians. With each intermarriage another Jewish family was swallowed up by the Christian community. The congregation which the German Jews had founded passed into the hands of the Jews from Russia, Rumania, Galicia, and the rest of Eastern Europe who brought to Canada not only religious doctrine but also a tradition closely connected with the dynamic Jewish life in Europe.

All the downtown synagogues were built by immigrants who had come from Eastern European countries like Russia, Poland, Rumania, Galicia, and Hungary. Only two synagogues, the B'nai Jacob and the Beth David, were purchased by the newcomers from Jews who had established themselves in this country many years earlier.

When immigrants arrived here thirty or forty years ago, their more established *landslayt* would recount the history of the Jewish community of Montreal, its synagogues and institutions. They would tell them about the Jewish families who had come from Eastern Europe thirty or forty years earlier and how these families were now well established in successful businesses. Montreal was still a small town, a *shtetl*, when they arrived penniless and without prospects. However, they met German Jews who offered friendship and assistance.

The German Jews already owned large businesses in Montreal. They dealt in dry goods, textiles, tobacco, leather, horses, and jewelry, conducting their businesses from Notre Dame, McGill, de la Commune, St. Paul and the neighbouring side streets. Russian and Rumanian Jews could communicate with the German Jews in German. The more well-to-do German Jews would help the newcomers from Eastern Europe to become storekeepers or peddlers. If the immigrants were tailors, the German Jews would assist them in opening small shops where they could produce inexpensive clothing, especially trousers. These modest shops grew into large modern clothing factories, each employing hundreds of workers.

Just as the first Jewish immigrants from Russia and Rumania depended on the German Jews when they first came to this country seventy or eighty years ago, so the German Jews had relied on the Spanish Jews when they arrived. When the German Jews became involved in building the Sha'ar Hashomayim Synagogue on Cadieux Street they took in the Russian and Polish Jews as partners. Later, when the wealthier German Jews moved uptown and built a synagogue on McGill College Avenue, the Russian Jews of the B'nai Jacob Congregation took over the synagogue on Cadieux Street, since known as the Russian shul. Similarly the Rumanian Jews founded the Beth David Congregation, taking over the Spanish and Portuguese Synagogue on Chénéville Street which then became the Rumanian shul.

No sooner did the immigrant begin to feel at home in the synagogue, than he wanted to have a say in synagogue affairs. At times this led to angry exchanges with the president or *gabai* which left the immigrant discontented. When a group of disaffected immigrants met, they would make plans for a new congregation where democracy and camaraderie would prevail, where *aliyahs* would be fairly distributed, where newcomers could assume responsible positions such as president, vice-president, or trustee. And so it came about that many small synagogues were founded by the immigrants. They were housed in buildings erected for this purpose or in old houses which were rented or purchased. Walking today along such downtown streets as Cadieux, St. Dominique, City Hall, de Montigny,[30] Dorchester, Lagauchetière and others, you may recognize many houses that once were synagogues. Some are now shops or small factories, while low-income families live in others. The congregations once housed in them have relocated to the Jewish neighbourhood, no longer in this part of town.

Sick Benefit Societies

THE SICK BENEFIT SOCIETIES of Montreal first came into existence about forty years ago. Many immigrants became members. Joining was easy and one *landsman* would bring in another. As no sick benefit societies had existed in the old country, it was necessary for *landslayt* to explain the concept to the newcomer.

"On this side of the Atlantic," they would say, "a person is alone even if he has relatives. If you fall ill, there is no one to look after you. Here everyone is concerned only with himself, hence the importance of joining a sick benefit society. Then someone will be there to take care of you if you get sick. The society sends a doctor and a committee of the society comes to visit. In addition, you receive weekly sick benefit payments . . ."

The *landslayt* offered other compelling reasons for becoming a member in a society. It provided an opportunity to meet people socially and form friendships. Someone with a talent for public speaking could become a secretary or vice-president and even ascend to the presidency. *Landslayt* would draw the newcomer's attention to certain individuals who had arrived penniless from Russia or Rumania not long ago and now held important positions in the society. One was a recording secretary, another a treasurer or even a president. All you needed was a silver tongue, and if you had good penmanship, you could advance quickly through the ranks.

When an immigrant decided to become a member of the society, he was first required to undergo a physical examination. The doctor had to determine if he was fit to be admitted into the society. This gave the immigrant his first opportunity to see what a Jewish doctor looked like in Canada. Usually the doctor was a young man who spoke to the immigrant in Yiddish. He wasted no time in assuring the immigrant with a smile that he was, thank God, strong and healthy and would undoubtedly be allowed to join the society. He would also give him words of encouragement that he would be "all right" in Canada, and reassured him that after he had worked hard and become established, he would experience pride and joy in his new life.

In the beginning, the meetings of the society seemed bizarre to the immigrant. The procedures and rituals were completely foreign to any he had witnessed in the old country. The speeches of the officers also sounded strange. Their sentences were a mixture of English, Yiddish, and German. However, he did enjoy the fact that the members referred to each other as "brothers". Hearing himself addressed as brother by a complete stranger, one who was obviously well established, made him feel truly at home even if the speeches of the officers did not sound like Yiddish and the proceedings were still alien. But he soon grew accustomed to the routine, especially when he discovered that the functionaries, the president, the vice-president, and the secretaries, were all recent immigrants like himself, tailors or cloakmakers, grocers or small businessmen, inhabiting the same streets as his friends and *landslayt*.

After a short time as a member of the society, he became friendly with the brothers. If he were timid or reserved, the brothers would endeavour to make him feel at ease. They spoke to him in a friendly manner, inquired about his problems, and gave him encouragement. If he were slaving away in a factory, they would say to him, "Here you need not be ashamed of your work . We all work . . . a worker is as important as anyone else . . ."

If he earned little they would tell him, "Be patient . . . take your time . . . you will be successful." They would name certain brothers who not long ago were poor and now, *keneynehore*, may the evil eye be averted, they owned their own houses and traveled by horse and buggy.

The officers would speak a Germanic form of Yiddish but only during the meetings. Before the official meetings and after they were over, they spoke English or Yiddish like all the other brothers. They urged the members to attend all the meetings as there was no greater pleasure than to spend an evening at a society meeting. They spoke with pity of those people who did not belong to a society. "Such people", they said, "are lonely and alone, lonely while they live and alone when they die. No one will care when they pass away. However, when a member of the society dies, even in the middle of the night, the secretary is awakened and informed. Even in a storm or blizzard, the secretary can always be reached. The secretary will notify everyone else, whomever should be notified. . . . Even in thunder and lightning everyone comes to the brother who has died. He is never left by himself. His funeral is arranged, a brotherly funeral. . . ."

And thus the officers expounded on the benefits of being a brother in the society.

To the newly arrived Jewish immigrant the sick benefit society meant a great deal. There he met all kinds of people, *landslayt* and friends. In their midst he felt like a brother among brothers. It was always fascinating to hear how the brothers earned a living as they were engaged in a variety of occupations. One was a sack salesman; a second peddled bananas and vegetables; a third travelled to the countryside to purchase animal hides, chickens, and eggs; a fourth was a sewing machine salesman; a fifth ran a junk shop in Point St. Charles or a second-hand shop on Craig Street or St. Antoine Street; a sixth was a grocer, and so on and so forth.

The brothers would offer advice and instruction to the newcomer on how to improve his situation in order to become established in the new world. If, for example, he were unhappy with factory work, they would advise him to leave the factory and instruct him as to how to become a self-employed businessman.

The grocer would tell him how easy it was to run a grocery store even without experience. People who in the old country were teachers or matchmakers had successfully opened their own grocery stores. They made a good living with no complaints.

The country peddler would advise the unhappy factory worker to go to a wholesaler, pick up some merchandise and go to the countryside. It made no difference which countryside. "Farmers are always the same, they are decent people. When a Jewish peddler arrives, they are always friendly. You can do business with them. You can communicate with them in sign language, with your hands. They put you up at night . . . with pleasure . . ."

The banana peddler would advise him to buy a horse and wagon and start peddling bananas and vegetables. "In this country," he would say, "there is no shame in riding around with a horse and wagon." He would point to himself. In the old country he had never even stood beside a horse. Here he learned how . . . there was nothing to it! He tried it and—thank God—he has already brought over his entire family, paid for all the steamship tickets, and makes a fine living. In the summer he sends his wife to the country, to St. Sophie or New Glasgow.[31] He has nothing against Christopher Columbus.

The brothers would explain to the newcomer how to leave the factory and go into business. To start a small business you needed capital, about $100 or $150. That amount could be borrowed from the Hebrew Free Loan Association (*Gmiles Khsodim*), if you had two guarantors, "endorsers." The brothers were very enthusiastic about the Free Loan Association and spoke with great respect about Mr. Z. Fineberg,[32] its founder, who lent out money for various purposes such as acquiring a horse and wagon for peddling, outfitting a grocery store, purchasing a sewing machine for a small tailor shop, or obtaining passage tickets for close relatives coming to Canada. The brothers would offer to act as guarantors for the newcomer's loan if he were prepared to begin his own business.

The information the immigrant received from the society brothers was extremely important. Many present-day businessmen who run companies worth tens or hundreds of thousands of dollars will recall that they or their fathers began those large companies on the advice of immigrant Jews with a start-up capital of $100 or $200 borrowed from friends, *landslayt*, or the Free Loan Association.

During the society's meeting various problems were discussed. One of the most common was the cemetery. In the course of this discussion the newcomer came to realize that even here, in Montreal, Jews still had to confront the problem of death. He discovered that once in a while a Jewish immigrant would die before he had had the opportunity to become financially successful and fully Canadian. A tailor or a cloakmaker died of consumption, which he had contracted while working in a sweatshop. A country peddler was killed when his horse and wagon were run over by a train at a railway crossing. On another occasion a bricklayer met his death when he fell off a high wall, his arms full of bricks. These incidents made a profound impression on the immigrant. He was even more keenly aware of the need for the protection of the society although he personally felt far from death and the cemetery. For someone who had recently arrived in this country and about to begin a new life, the idea of the cemetery was the furthest from his mind.

In the society he would encounter one brother who appeared more intelligent, aristocratic, educated, and Canadianized than the rest. This brother could be seen engaging in friendly conversation with everyone and even sought out the newcomer. He spoke to him about an intriguing subject—insurance.

This brother, of course, was an insurance agent. He made it clear to the immigrant that a brother in the society provided with sick benefits and cemetery plots, is nonetheless alone and vulnerable without an insurance policy. The insurance company takes a small payment and in return, when the insured dies, even the next day, his family receives a large sum of money—

one thousand dollars in cash—a fortune. If someone survives for twenty years, he himself receives a large sum of money during his lifetime. It was difficult for the immigrant to refuse the insurance agent who had spoken with such friendliness and persistence. To the immigrant the insurance agent appeared to be his best friend who was more concerned than anyone else about his fate and his future. Again he went to the doctor for a physical examination to determine if he qualified for an insurance policy. After having obtained the insurance policy, he felt more at ease, secure, protected, and connected to the new life in the new world.

G.H. Beaulieu and Joseph Fineberg, 1159 Ontario Street,
1903. Zigmond Fineberg (1863-1967), whose name appears in
the shop window, founded the Hebrew Free
Loan Association in 1911.
Courtesy of the Canadian Jewish Congress Archives.

At the *Arbeiter Ring* (Workmen's Circle)

MANY OF THE JEWISH immigrants who were attracted to radical politics, or whose friends or relatives were radicals, joined the *Arbeiter Ring*. The *Arbeiter Ring* provided the same benefits as the sick benefit society but an entirely different social environment. At the beginning of the century, militant socialists, anarchists, and other "enlightened workers" belonged to the *Arbeiter Ring*. Its officers and members were mainly factory workers with the odd businessman who spoke and acted like the workers.

In the *Arbeiter Ring* immigrants arriving in Montreal after 1905 would meet Jews who had taken part in the revolution against the Russian czar, manning the barricades in Minsk, Vilna and other cities in the Pale of Settlement. Many had been in czarist prisons or had escaped while being transported to Siberia and made their way to Montreal where they became tailors, cloakmakers, and small businessmen.

Younger immigrants, former adherents of the *Bund* and other socialist organizations in the cities and towns of their native Russia, who had witnessed or participated in the failed revolution of 1905, felt most at home in the *Arbeiter Ring*. Here they found almost the same atmosphere which had prevailed in the revolutionary circles of the old country.

The leaders of the *Arbeiter Ring* were, in theory at least, bitter opponents of an organized Jewish community, as were some of the members. They had a negative attitude to orthodox Judaism and religion in general. They strongly opposed any kind of Zionist activity. Devout believers in internationalism, their sacred slogan was "workers of the world unite!"

A new member of the *Arbeiter Ring* often heard lectures and speeches on socialist themes. In those days socialist leaders believed that once the struggle for the forty-four-hour work week was won, a social revolution would follow. Therefore the forty-four-hour work week became a priority for the socialists.

At social gatherings the members of the *Arbeiter Ring* used to sing songs from the revolution of 1905 in Yiddish or Russian. Popular among the Russian songs was the revolutionary prison song *"Solntze voskhodit i zakhodit a v'tyurme mayi tyomna*" ("The sun rises and sets but my prison cell is in darkness"). During many of these social occasions money was collected to support Russian revolutionaries languishing in prison.

Russian revolutionary traditions were dear to the hearts of the socialists. May Day was an important holiday which was celebrated with a parade to the Champs de Mars followed by a concert and mass meeting in the Labour Temple or in Prince Arthur Hall.[33] The parade would stream down Main Street but the marchers were mainly Jewish workers. In later years greater numbers of workers from different ethnic groups participated. On the Champs de Mars the marchers would separate into various nationality groups so that each group could conduct its own special open air meeting. The Jewish group was always the most impressive and the largest. In their own languages the speakers would emphasize the importance of uniting the workers of all countries and fighting for a forty-four-hour work week. The belief that the workers of the world could be united was shared by all the members of the *Arbeiter Ring* and socialist sympathizers until the outbreak of the Great War in 1914 when European workers fought against each other.

Radical influences on the members of the *Arbeiter Ring* emanated from New York by way of the daily newspaper the *Jewish Daily Forward* (*Forverts*), which was militantly radical, and the weekly *Freie Arbeiter Shtime* (Voice of the Free Worker), the organ of the Jewish anarchists in America.[34] On occasion radical speakers would come to lecture on socialist and anarchist themes.

The Jewish immigrants who became members of the *Arbeiter Ring* were astonished to learn that here in Canada, where there was no czar, where everyone was free to do as he pleased and where there was no discrimination against Jews, there were as many socialist writers, poets, and orators as in Russia. They discovered that associated with the *Forward*, the *Freie Arbeiter Shtime*, and the *Zukunft* were groups of socialist theorists and writers who wrote, thought, and spoke exactly as though they were still living in Russia and participating in the ongoing revolutionary struggle against the czar.

A number of these writers and speakers were in fact recent immigrants who not long ago were engaged in revolutionary activity against the czar in Minsk or Vilna or Warsaw and had fled the old country to escape the czarist prisons. Others had come to America many years earlier, well before the inception of the 1905 revolution. Almost all the radical writers believed that joining forces against religion and eliminating national sentiment among the Jewish masses would hasten the advent of the social revolution. This belief was shattered in later years, especially during the Great War, when most of the radical writers of the *Forward* and the other radical newspapers and journals became more preoccupied with the pressing problem of Jewish rescue than with the abstract ideal of internationalism and the struggle to unite the workers of the world for the social revolution.

Bloody Sunday, January 22, 1905, St. Petersburg.
From *An Introduction to Russian History and Culture*
by Ivan Spector, Van Nostrand Company, 1949.

Among the Poor

LIFE IN THE JEWISH COMMUNITY was far from peaceful during the period of intensive immigration. Immigrants always found reasons to quarrel. There was an ongoing struggle between the "uptown" and the "downtown." The downtowners were the newly established Jews who sought to increase their influence in the life of the Jewish community. The uptowners were determined to maintain their ascendancy and eyed the downtown Jews with distrust.

The downtowners were split into several factions. Various political groups were constantly feuding over issues which surfaced in the Jewish neighbourhood. The difficulties of those days seem trivial and inconsequential compared to the problems confronting the Jews of today. In religious circles the conflicts usually involved arguments over kosher meat, altercations between rabbis and *shokhtim,* those who slaughtered the animals. Among secular Jews disputes tended to be over the application of abstract social philosophy or theories of nationalism to everyday Jewish life.

In addition, there was the perpetual class struggle between the workers and their employers. The majority of the workers were embittered by poverty and misfortune. Many were employed in the needle trades, while others worked as unskilled labourers. Unskilled labour was in great demand, especially in construction where prior to the invention of the steam shovel, workers were required to dig foundations. Many Jewish workers were employed in construction either as unskilled labourers or as qualified tradesmen. The unskilled workers earned very little, but many of the skilled construction workers were able to work their way up and become successful building contractors who erected important buildings in our city.

Many Jewish workers lived in dire poverty. Those with large families suffered the most. If a worker had a wife who was healthy, hard-working and a good cook, his situation could be ameliorated. He could rent a larger flat and take in boarders. This meant hard work for his wife, but it made a significant difference in their financial situation. With the income from the boarders he could meet his expenses and also save a few dollars.

Tailors and cloakmakers used to earn much more than unskilled workers. They were also better dressed, of course, and lived in somewhat more attractive accommodations. Whereas unskilled labourers for the most part inhabited the small streets around Craig and Notre Dame, where their rent was eight or ten dollars a month, tailors resided further north, between Dorchester and Ontario, from St. Urbain to Sanguinet. The better paid tailors lived north of Sherbrooke Street, up to Duluth Street, where the monthly rent was between twelve and fifteen dollars a month.

Although tailors and cloakmakers earned more than the other workers, their work was seasonal. Several weeks, or sometimes even months, could go by between one season and the next during which they earned nothing. They then became as poor as the other workers.

In the weeks when there was no work, they became indebted to grocers, butchers, and *landslayt*. When their work resumed, they had to repay the debts of the slack period. It often happened that the working season was short, so short that it ended before the tailors could pay off their debts and they were compelled to borrow all over again.

In those years when Jewish workers wrestled with the problems of poverty, they could not provide for their children. They could neither buy them decent, warm clothing nor give them a proper education. Very few tailors, cloakmakers, bakers, and unskilled labourers could afford to send their children to high school. In most cases they sent their children to work at thirteen or fourteen years of age. It was hard to find a job for a small thirteen-year-old girl, but one could always manage to find something for a boy. He would become a newsboy, selling the city's daily newspapers on the street for one cent apiece.

Many young boys could be seen running up and down St. Catherine Street, St. James, Notre Dame, and other major thoroughfares selling newspapers. These were Jewish boys, sons of tailors, cloakmakers, and un-skilled workers. Summer and winter they sold newspapers, and the few pennies they brought home helped their parents make ends meet. During a strike, many families lived solely on the small change these children earned as newsboys. Thanks to their experience selling newspapers, many of these boys acquired business skills which they used later as adults, opening small businesses to avoid becoming workers like their fathers. Often these small businesses expanded into large companies. Many of today's businessmen will recall that around forty years ago they began their careers as newsboys.

Class Divisions

DURING THE ERA of mass immigration, while workers struggled with poverty and need, class boundaries were sharply defined. This was evident everywhere in the life of the Jewish community.

Workers played a prominent role in the community but as a separate class. They were in constant conflict with non-workers over all issues, even those which had nothing to do with class interest. When a meeting of all the organizations and societies was convened to deal with an issue of concern to the entire community, the representatives of the workers' organizations conducted themselves as a separate entity and spoke entirely differently from the other delegates, whom they considered "bourgeois." They would hold forth at length about socialism and quote from socialist theoreticians even when the debate was about trivial matters. Many of the non-socialist delegates would hear them out respectfully, while others would lose patience and attack them.

The worker groups clashed among themselves. The ongoing ideological struggle was keenly felt in the Jewish neighbourhood. The three groups who would constantly vie for influence over the immigrant Jewish workers were the anarchists, the socialists, and the Labour Zionists (*Poalei Tsionistn*). In the beginning the anarchists were the strongest group and the Labour Zionists the weakest. The principal rivals of the anarchists were the socialists, while the Labour Zionists were too weak to compete. Later the situation changed as the Labour Zionists grew in strength and the anarchists went into decline. When this happened, bitter strife ensued between the socialists and the Labour Zionists, with the anarchists too weak to participate.

The point of contention was how the world was to be restructured the day after the social revolution. The anarchists, the socialists, and the Labour Zionists all firmly believed in the coming of the revolution and that it was the task of the world proletariat in general and the tailors and cloakmakers in particular to hasten its arrival. However, the question remained: What was to be done on the day after the revolution? How was the life of the workers to be organized in a world without capitalism?

The anarchists demanded a free society without governments and the governed. The socialists argued that after the revolution a socialist state and a socialist police force would be necessary to maintain order. The Labour Zionists agreed with the need for a state in a socialist society but they insisted that a socialist state would not solve the Jewish question. The socialists countered that in a socialist state where all people were equal, the Jewish question would be automatically resolved.

Traditional Jews were terrified of the anarchists and regarded them as dangerous enemies of the Jewish people. They claimed that the anarchists, who agitated for free love, had no respect for accepted moral standards. Although the socialists were also worlds apart ideologically from the traditional Jews, there was no acrimony between them. The socialists mingled more with ordinary Jewish immigrants. They were active in the union where they came into contact with orthodox Jews who were loyal supporters. They were much more tolerant than the anarchists.

The socialists had an extensive press. Their main publication, the *Jewish Daily Forward* (the *Forverts*), had always sought to win over the ordinary Jewish immigrants. With the help of the *Forward*, the socialists were able to have a strong influence on the Jewish workers. For a long time the *Forward* had been printing extremely anti-Zionist articles which attacked Eretz Israel as a country and Zionism as a movement for being based on anti-socialist principles. The Labour Zionists fought hard to defend Eretz Israel, the Land of Israel, as a suitable country for colonization and Zionism as a movement that was not incompatible with socialism.

A Poalei Zion banner designed by Todres Geller.
"As the Labour Zionists grew in strength the anarchists
went into decline."

The Extremists

THE MOST EXTREME of the Jewish radicals in the period of mass immigration were the anarchists. Anarchists had made their appearance in Montreal before the beginning of this century. Many came directly from Eastern Europe. Others, arriving from England or New York, spoke English fluently and were well versed in English radical literature. They were more influenced by Western European radicalism than by the Russian revolutionary movement.

Some of the anarchists who came to Montreal from New York were brought over by large firms as experts and first-class tradesmen in certain needle trades such as cloaks and waists.[35] The waist industry, which in America was one of the most important of the clothing trades, was beginning to grow. In those days it was fashionable for girls and young women to wear skirts and waists instead of dresses. The waist was the height of fashion. A girl would only wear a full dress if she were attending a wedding. A bride might wear a wedding gown, but the next day she would dress up in a pretty blouse and skirt, or in a suit made in a cloak shop.

When the garment industry in Montreal was in its infancy, first class artisans such as designers, cutters, and foremen were not available in this country. They had to be imported from New York which had become a major centre for these trades. The designers and foremen who came from New York worked here for a short time, and after saving a little money, opened their own shops, becoming manufacturers in competition with the bosses who had brought them here.

These skilled workers brought with them to Montreal the stormy radicalism of New York. Many were anarchists and naturally some of them were socialists. The Labour Zionists were not yet known in the last years of the previous century. The anarchists of that time were interested in Jewish life only insofar as they could disseminate their atheistic and anti-nationalist propaganda among the Jewish masses. Among them were those who in their youth had studied in the yeshivas of Eastern Europe, had been extremely pious, but were influenced by the anti-religious propaganda preached by the Hebrew writers of the Haskalah (the Jewish Enlightenment) in the 1870s and 1880s. A number of the socialist activists were also former yeshiva students, who had left the yeshivas under the sway of the Haskalah writers. Having embraced socialism or anarchism, they completely rejected not only the yeshiva environment but also the Hebrew Haskalah writers and their secular nationalist followers in Europe who were the forerunners of modern Zionism. There were exceptions. Many socialist writers and poets in their later years began to delve into Jewish sources and write about figures from ancient Jewish literature and early Hebrew poets and moralists, who were among the pillars of Jewish tradition and history.

In Montreal the anarchists carried out their propaganda work by distributing the *Freie Arbeiter Shtime* (Voice of the Free Worker)[36] as well as anarchist pamphlets, and by bringing in lecturers from New York. Older radicals will recall that the anarchists organized the first May Day parade in Montreal. In this connection they tell the following story. One of the anarchist leaders, a waist manufacturer, became perturbed when he realized that the first May Day parade could not be characterized as internationalist as the only participants were Jews. In those days there were a few poor Italians in Montreal, one of whom was an organ grinder who used to play his barrel organ on the street. The anarchist approached him offering a whole dollar if he would march in the May Day parade. The Italian accepted the offer, put away his barrel organ, and marched in the parade. That day the anarchists and socialists were jubilant. They proclaimed that an organ grinder was also a worker and a member of the proletariat. The parade thus became internationalist, in keeping with the slogan "workers of the world unite."

Another story is told about the same manufacturer which is also characteristic of the anarchists of that era. The manufacturer and his business partner, also an anarchist, believed in the class struggle. For that reason they oppressed their workers. They wanted the workers to become class conscious and militant. When the workers complained, the anarchist bosses would say to them: "If you want to improve your situation you must organize a union."

After the union was organized, the owners bragged to their friends and comrades about their great accomplishment—raising the consciousness of their workers. When the union demanded improved working conditions, the anarchist bosses replied, "Only through a strike can a union win concessions for the workers." The union called a strike.

The anarchist bosses were pleased and boasted to their friends and comrades that their workers had become militant, they were on strike. When the workers picketed the factory, the anarchist bosses called the police to disperse the workers. The strikers fought the police and the bosses again boasted to their radical friends and comrades, "We have achieved great things. We have caused the workers to become revolutionaries, to fight the police." Only after the workers had demonstrated that they were desperately embittered did the bosses reach an agreement with the union.

The First Socialists

THE FIRST SOCIALISTS made their appearance in Montreal at the turn of the century. At first they attracted little attention. The immigrant Jews arriving in the early 1900s had only the vaguest notion of the socialist platform. On a superficial level they had heard that the socialists opposed the divisions between rich and poor and wanted a society based on equality without class distinctions. To the average immigrant this seemed impossible.

Soon after, when revolution was raging throughout the Russian Empire at the time of the Russo-Japanese war, Jewish immigrants heard more about socialism. They took a keen interest in the revolution and the war which Japan was waging against Russia. Their hatred of the czar was so intense that they rejoiced at every setback suffered by the czar's army despite their awareness of the fact that Jews served in that army. In fact, many Jewish soldiers took the opportunity to escape and emigrate to the United States or Canada.

The immigrants cherished the hope that the socialists in Russia would overthrow the czarist regime and introduce universal freedom and equality. Their antipathy toward the czarist regime was not only based on the fact that it tolerated anti-Jewish pogroms, but also because Russia was the only country with restrictive laws against Jews. Russian Jews were not allowed to reside in designated parts of the Russian Empire, nor were they permitted to engage in certain occupations and professions. Jewish immigrants arriving in Canada were overjoyed to discover that public opinion on this side of the ocean was hostile to Russia. Even the socialists had great respect for the multi-millionaire capitalist Jacob Schiff[37] because his bank had loaned huge sums of money to Japan to finance the war against the czar.

Jewish immigrants did not believe that the socialists would be able to transform society or even to wrest the factories and sweatshops from the capitalists and nationalize them. They were convinced, however, that socialists in the United States and Canada could help the Russian socialists and revolutionaries to overthrow the czar. They were also confident that the socialists could organize the impoverished tailors and cloakmakers into unions to fight for better working conditions in factories and sweatshops, for shorter hours, higher wages, and for fewer bosses instead of the foreman, the contractor, the subcontractor, the subsubcontractor, and so on.[38]

When the socialists spoke to the immigrant workers about Marxism, the abolition of private property and the redistribution of wealth, the latter were skeptical. To them it sounded like a fantastic utopia. But when the socialists talked about eliminating subcontractors and obtaining higher wages and a shorter work day, the immigrants became wildly enthusiastic. Similarly, speeches about the struggle against czarism and for freedom and equal rights for Jews elicited a warm response.

The first task of the Jewish socialists in Montreal was to circulate the *Jewish Daily Forward*. The *Forward* was the first Yiddish newspaper to be "peddled" in Montreal and its first peddler was H. Hershman[39] who continues to be the distributor of the *Forward* and other Yiddish newspapers.

Before Hershman brought the *Forward* to Montreal, only a small number of Jews in the city read a Yiddish newspaper, the *Tageblatt*. This newspaper was mailed to subscribers who had been signed up by its agent, Wilensky, the first Jewish bookseller in Montreal. Wilensky's store was on De Bullion Street, then Cadieux Street, near Dorchester, where, in addition to religious items such as *shir-hamalesn* (leaflets for use as amulets during childbirth), *tsitses* (fringed undergarments worn by religious Jews), *tefillin* (phylacteries), and *taleysim* (prayer shawls), one could also purchase soft-covered Yiddish novels printed in New York.

The *Tageblatt*, as I mentioned already, was only available to subscribers. The first to sell door to door making it possible for everyone to buy and read a Yiddish newspaper was H. Hershman with the *Jewish Daily Forward*. His aim was not profit, but simply to disseminate socialist propaganda.

Hershman was a young cloakmaker who made cloaks by day and distributed the *Forward* in the evening. When his career as a cloakmaker came to an abrupt end—he lost his job—the socialists decided that Hershman should give up cloaks and devote himself full-time to the *Forward*. It was also agreed that the *Forward* should not be sold door to door, but from a shop on Main Street. At that time it was easy to rent a store on Main Street if one were willing to pay the price, which was then about five dollars a month. The socialists determined that if a partner could be found to pay half the rent for the store, namely two dollars and fifty cents, they could afford to take a chance.

And they did. They found a shoemaker who agreed to rent the store in partnership with the socialists for five dollars a month. The store was on Main Street near Ontario. And this was how the first store for Yiddish newspapers and books opened in Montreal.

Founding of the Jewish Socialist Party of America
and Canada, Rochester, New York, 1911.
Archives of Ontario F1405-23-17, MSR 1504-1

The First Jewish Bookstore

WHEN IN 1902 the socialists opened a store on Main Street to sell the *Jewish Daily Forward*, they in effect created a cultural centre, the first Jewish cultural centre in Montreal. In addition to the *Forward*, the store sold other Yiddish newspapers from New York as well as the best Yiddish literature then available in America. Hershman's bookstore became the central gathering place of the immigrant Jewish intellectuals. They would come there not only to purchase newspapers but to debate world affairs or party politics.

The Jewish bookstore greatly enhanced the beauty and grandeur of Main Street in the eyes of the immigrant Jews. To them Main Street between Ontario and Craig was the most attractive and interesting street in Montreal. It was also their walking street. On a Friday evening Jewish immigrants would stroll along Main Street. They were intrigued and impressed by the window displays in the large stores. Walking by a clothing store, they would eagerly examine the new suits in the window. For six and a half or seven dollars one could buy a blue serge suit which was elegant and genuinely American. In the old country, even the wealthy did not wear such elegant suits.

In another shop window they would study men's hats. In the summer the entire window was filled with straw hats which cost about forty or fifty cents a piece. In fall or winter, the derby hat made its appearance. In the old country only rich men, prominent merchants, matchmakers, itinerant preachers, and other pious people wore stiff felt hats similar to the derby on Saturdays. Here in Montreal even workers wore them, and in the middle of the week. For ninety-eight cents, or a dollar and ten cents, one could buy a derby hat.

Passing a shoe store, the immigrants would inspect the latest shoes. For a dollar and seventy-five cents or two dollars, one could purchase a stylish pair of tan shoes with long narrow pointed toes in true American style. Even black shoes which cost twenty or thirty cents less than the tan shoes, appeared sporty and stylish compared to the shoes worn in the old country.

Of greatest interest to the women were the windows in the millinery store. They would scrutinize the latest styles of women's hats, especially the large feathers on the hats. The hat itself was important, but more important was the feather. The longer the feather, the more beautiful and impressive the hat. When women met to discuss matters of special interest to them, much of the talk was about the feathers on their hats.

Both men and women would stop in front of the window of the photography studio and take note of the various poses in the photographs on display. At that time immigrants often went to photographers to have pictures taken which they could send to the old country to show their relatives and friends how Americanized they had become. They took their first pictures dressed in American clothes, a man in a blue serge suit, a Derby hat or a straw hat, with tan pointy shoes, and a woman with a large feather on her hat.

Walking along Main Street they would also stop in front of Hershman's bookstore, a spot which was reminiscent of Jewish life in the old country. The merchandise displayed in the window consisted of Yiddish books and pamphlets. Most Jewish immigrants of that era were not avid readers but, nevertheless, from time to time they would buy a small book.

Novels by Shomer,[40] Tannenbaum,[41] Blaustein and Seifert[42] accounted for a great many of the books. There were also translations from the Russian of novels by Tolstoy including *Anna Karenina* and *The Kreutzer Sonata*. The works of Emil Zola were translated from the French although Zola was known to Jewish immigrants not for his novels, but for the central role he played in the Dreyfus case.[43]

Among the pamphlets were historical accounts of the Dreyfus case, Chmielnicki,[44] the Spanish Inquisition, the bans of Rabbenu Gershom,[45] Shabbetai Tzevi,[46] and Bar Kokhba.[47] There were pamphlets written by doctors especially for girls and young women.

The immigrants also used to buy pamphlets by unknown authors who told exciting tales of adventure and high drama. One pamphlet told of a princess lost in the woods who was kidnapped by robbers and taken to a strange land where she was forced to work as a servant until it was learned that she was the daughter of royalty—a princess. Another pamphlet by the same author was about a duke who fell in love with a Jewish servant girl, an orphan, and carried her off to a distant land where she became a princess and helped the Jews who lived there.

There were also pamphlets about Cossacks. One described how a Cossack converted to Judaism and eventually became a Hasid. In a second pamphlet the same author told of a Hasid who strayed from the right path, converted to Christianity and over time became a Cossack.

There were a considerable number of political pamphlets, both socialist and anarchist. These, however, did not appeal to the average Jewish immigrant. Only enlightened socialists and anarchists would buy them. The socialists and anarchists were also familiar with the first-class Yiddish writers and poets in America such as Morris Winchevsky,[48] Z. Libin,[49] Jacob Gordin,[50] Morris Rosenfeld,[51] Leon Kobrin,[52] David Edelstadt,[53] Phillip Krantz,[54] and A. Liesen.[55] Ordinary immigrants had heard little about these writers. Several years later, after the upheavals of 1905 and 1906, Jews arriving in Montreal began to show more interest in the better Yiddish writers and poets of America and Europe, whose books were becoming available at Hershman's and in the other bookstores which later opened on Main Street.

Hirsch Hershman.
"Hershman's bookstore became the central gathering place of immigrant Jewish intellectuals."
Photo by Peter O. Gulkin. Courtesy of Sylvia Lustgarten.

The Second Jewish Bookstore

WHEN ONLY ONE Jewish bookstore existed on Main Street, it was frequented not only by lovers of literature and books but also by devotees of radical politics. Although in 1903 and 1904 both groups were small, they later grew significantly.

In those early years, radicals of all persuasions were interested in anti-religious literature. On display in the window of Hershman's bookstore were atheistic pamphlets and brochures whose brazenly provocative titles deeply offended traditional Jews. When religious immigrants saw these pamphlets in the window they were incredulous. Some thought they were the work of missionaries and began to suspect that missionaries were involved in the store. They would enter the store, buy a glass of soda water, and with furtive glances in all directions convince themselves that this was not a business run by missionaries.

There was a time, however, when these heretical booklets would disappear from the window. That was a few weeks before Rosh Hashana, the Jewish new year, when several kinds of new year's cards—large, larger, and very large—suddenly materialized in the display window. There were new year's cards that looked like great paper buildings. Others were in the shape of ocean liners complete with captain, sailors and life belts, carrying blessings for a good year from the American Jew to his relative in Europe with the wish that soon the European relative would embark on a ship bound for the free countries of the United States and Canada.

Another card depicted a synagogue with a *bima* (podium), a *Torah*, and an *ornkoydesh* (holy ark). On the *bima* stood patriarchal Jews wearing top hats. This card was meant to convey the notion that amidst the freedom and affluence of America, Jewish religious observance was alive and well.

In the weeks before Rosh Hashana few sales of socialist literature were made in the socialist bookstore. On the other hand, there was a brisk business in new year's cards. Everyone bought them—those on their way to becoming Canadianized as well as the newcomers. The more successful Jews would buy the larger, more impressive cards. The poorer Jews bought the smaller ones, but even the small cards could be folded and unfolded like accordions. When Jews would come to purchase new year's cards they usually bought other religious items at the same time, such as a prayer book for the High Holidays or a Jewish calendar, and while they were at it, they would inquire about *tsitses,* a *kine,* and a *menorah* for Chanukah. The customer reasoned that since he was already buying Jewish items, he might as well stock up for the year.

Although some radicals sharply criticized Hershman for dealing in such articles, he did not heed their criticism. Committed radicals were disappointed in him and began to hope for a second bookstore without religious articles where the atmosphere would be more in keeping with the spirit of internationalism and radicalism.

The religious atmosphere in Hershman's store only lasted for the duration of the High Holidays. When the holidays were over, the religious items were stored away on the shelves in the back until the next year. In the window again appeared the heretical pamphlets of B. Feigenbaum[56] and anti-religious brochures translated from the French. Socialist brochures, like Paul Lafargue's[57] *Le Droit à la paresse,* again made their appearance. But the devout radicals were already disillusioned with Hershman's store which increasingly became like any other store catering to the immigrant Jews on Main Street.

These hard-line radicals did not have long to wait. A second bookstore opened on Main Street exclusively for radical literature. Unofficial competition arose between the two bookstores, not commercial competition but ideological.

Only the hard-liners frequented the second bookstore whereas the first bookstore was patronized by intellectuals who were not radicals. While in the second bookstore socialist and anarchist theories and radical party politics were debated, in the first bookstore world politics were discussed. Nevertheless, it was not long before the second bookstore began to sell new year's cards, silk prayer shawls, and other religious articles.

Again the extreme radicals felt betrayed. Once more radical extremism was forced to retreat under the pressure of traditional Judaism exerted by the immigrant Jews on Main Street. The stronger the pressure of the immigrants, the fewer the sales of heretical anti-religious pamphlets, and the less one heard about the anti-religious escapades of the most extreme radicals, the anarchists, which in those days included festivities on Yom

Kippur, the Day of Atonement.

As the Jewish population grew, the extreme radicals lost their influence and the community developed other interests. Groups were formed devoted to non-partisan literature, poetry, and theatre. In both the first and second bookstores the works of well-known Jewish writers and poets from America and Europe became available, including books by Mendele Mocher Sforim,[58] Sholom Aleichem,[59] Peretz,[60] Dinesohn,[61] Frug,[62] and other early classical Russian Yiddish authors.

Mendele Mocher Sforim, Sholom Aleichem, Ben-Ami,
and Chaim Nachman Bialik.
Jewish Observer, London, Ontario.

Hebraists

Among the immigrants who arrived in the early years of this century there were also Hebraists, or, as they referred to themselves, *Hovevei Sfat Ever* (Lovers of the Hebrew Language). Some were elderly people who had come to Canada as children many years before and, after establishing themselves to a certain extent, were able to send steamship tickets to their parents. Others were middle-aged Jews, *maskilim* and teachers who in the old country had been scholarly young men,[63] *"eydems af kest,"*[64] supported by their wives' families. When the stipulated period for financial support ended they found themselves without prospects. They lacked the means to go into business and to become a worker was beneath their dignity. So they travelled to Canada where they could work without embarrassment. They set out with the idea that this was a land of work.

Among the Hebraists were also young men of eighteen to twenty years of age who came to Canada either because they had lost the desire to study in yeshiva or to avoid being conscripted into the czar's army. Interest in yeshiva studies waned under the influence of the Hebrew writers of the Haskalah[65] whose books circulated among yeshiva students at that time.

The Hebraists were quiet, reserved people who shunned boisterous social activities. They lived in a romantic Hebrew world, a world of Hebrew books and journals. In the old country the older and middle-aged Hebraists had been in the habit of reading *Hamelitz* (The Advocate)[66] and especially *Hatsfirah* (Dawn)[67] where they delighted in Sokolov's[68] *Divrei Hayamim* (Chronicles) containing commentaries on contemporary political issues. Younger Hebraists were enthralled by the novels of Smolenskin[69] and Mapu[70] and the poetry of Yehuda Leib Gordon.[71] Others were influenced by the cultural-historical articles of Achad Ha'am,[72] Lilienblum[73] and Joseph Gedalia Klausner[74] in *HaShiloah*,[75] the most important journal of the Hebrew-speaking intelligentsia in Russia.

When the immigrant Hebraists went for a walk on Main Street, they would stop in front of the Jewish bookstore, examine the books in the window, then go in to inquire about various Hebrew books. Former yeshiva students wanted to buy books such as those by Micah Joseph Berdishevsky,[76] Bershadsky's[77] *Neged Hazerem* (Against the Current),[78] Feierberg's[79] *Le'an* (Whither), and David Frischman's[80] translations of historical novels.

A young man would explain that before he left for Canada he had read a part of Smolenskin's *Ha To'eh Bdarchei Hachaim* (The Vagabond on the Roads of Life), and now wished to finish it. In fact, he was prepared to buy all of Smolenskin's books. A second wanted to buy all the poems of Yehuda Leib Gordon, while another was eager to purchase the *History of the Jews* by Graetz[81] translated into Hebrew in several thick volumes.

Many Hebraists wanted to buy annual sets of *Olam Katan* (Small World), a Hebrew language journal especially for children. Through this journal they hoped to awaken their grandchildren to the beauty of the Hebrew language and were prepared to pay any price for it.

However, in Hershman's bookstore there were no Hebrew books. Hershman was interested in socialist books, not Hebrew ones. When he saw that Jewish intellectuals were willing to pay five or ten dollars or more for Hebrew books, he tried to interest them in the less expensive socialist books. He offered them books by Marx and Kautsky,[82] Lassalle[83] and Bebel[84] as well as other socialist thinkers and theorists. But the Hebraists remained unreceptive to the radical literature.

The socialist Hershman sympathized with the Hebraists and their thirst for Hebrew books and began to respect the names of the Hebrew writers whose books the Hebraists requested. Together with the demand for secular Hebrew books, there was a call for religious books such as *Mishnayes*, *Khok leYisroel*, *Gemara*, and *Eyn Ya'akov*. At that point Hershman decided that it was necessary to open a store that specialized in Hebrew books and religious texts. He opened a store in partnership with the Hebraist and teacher Mendel Leib Sack.[85] Well-known in cultural circles, Sack was one of the founders of the Labour Zionist movement in the city.

The new store, situated on Main Street near De Montigny, was called the Ezra Bookstore. It became a central meeting place for Hebraists and *maskilim*. All the Hebrew books available in New York were sold there as well as Hebrew books imported from Europe.

However, the venture was short-lived. Commercially it was a failure. For Sack, the Hebrew pedagogue and principal of the Talmud Torah in the Baron de Hirsch Institute, it was not worthwhile to devote himself full-time to the store.

The closing of the Ezra Bookstore was a tremendous loss to the Hebraists. Yet, although they had lost their meeting place, they were no longer as alone and isolated as before. They had made contacts in New York where it was possible to obtain Hebrew books and journals and where influential Hebrew poets and writers were already resident. Among the Hebrew writers arriving in New York during the period of mass immigration was Reuben Brainin who exerted every effort to develop a modern Hebrew press there. By the time Brainin came to Montreal in 1912 to be the editor of the *Keneder Adler*, there was already a significant group of Hebraists which included committed Zionists and Hebrew teachers dedicated to the cause of Hebrew education in Montreal.

Reuben Brainin became the editor of the *Keneder Adler*
in 1912.

Crisis

Most of the immigrant Jews left the old country to escape poverty and need. In emigrating to the United States or Canada, they were certain that they would be settling in a land of peace and plenty. Therefore they were terribly shocked and painfully disappointed when upon their arrival they found themselves in the midst of an economic crisis.[86] They encountered deprivation and destitution at every turn, whether among new immigrants or those who had been in the country for some time. It was tragic to witness the immigrants arriving during the depression [of 1907-08] confused and helpless. Christopher Columbus became the target of a barrage of curses as the impoverished Jews questioned why they had come to the new land.

Everyone was looking for work, the newcomers as well as the old-timers. The factories were closed, the sweatshops boarded up. An eerie silence reigned. How long would the crisis last? When would it end? What had caused it? These were the questions which the immigrants would ask one another when they met in Dufferin Park, on the mountain or elsewhere. They would encounter their friends and *landslayt* not only on Saturdays or Sundays but on weekdays as well.

Married immigrants who needed to send a few dollars to their families in the old country every week suffered the most. A married man was at a loss to explain to his wife why he was not sending her any money. He did not know what to advise her. How would she survive this time of crisis when he earned nothing or perhaps just the three or four dollars a week he required for his own subsistence?

Writing home was a difficult task for the immigrants. While they had been able to send money it had not been so bad. Then they could write a short note, or, if they were unable to write themselves, they could ask a friend or *landsman* to write for them. But when they had to pour out their hearts and explain to their wives in a far-off *shtetl* how bitterly they suffered in the "golden land," how hard it was to earn a penny—such a letter was extremely difficult to compose. Some immigrants went to Tatarinsky. To poor illiterate immigrants he was a good friend. He kept an "address bureau" and was generous with his advice to needy immigrants. Those who sought his help considered him to be a writer, a sage, an orator, and a politician.

Immigrant Jews did not understand the true cause of the economic recession, nor did they know how long it would last. Those who had been in Canada longer would try to provide an explanation. Some would say that it was because the workers worked long hours producing more merchandise than was needed. When a surplus of merchandise accumulated in the wholesales and in the retail stores, the factories had to be closed until the accumulated surplus was depleted.

Others explained that it had to do with the elections in the United States. The capitalists, they said, locked up their factories to create a crisis in the country and thereby convince the workers not to vote for the government but for the opposition party which the capitalists hoped would better serve their interests.

The first to suffer from the economic crisis were the workers, but when the workers could no longer pay their bills at the grocer's and the butcher's, everyone felt its impact. The grocers, the butchers, and the landlords suffered, but not as keenly as the workers. The grocers, butchers, and bakers made contributions to the soup kitchens set up to feed the Jewish immigrants who were destitute. The soup kitchens were organized by Eastern European Jews, *landslayt* or immigrants who were already somewhat Canadianized. But the victims of the depression went to the soup kitchens only as a last resort.

Many immigrants tried to escape the depression by moving to another city. People migrated from one part of Canada to another and from Canada to the United States and vice versa. From Montreal Jewish immigrants went to Toronto, Hamilton or Ottawa, hoping the crisis would be less severe in smaller centres. From Ottawa, Hamilton, and Toronto people came to Montreal in the belief that in a larger city they would find some protection from the depression.

During this critical period Jewish immigrant workers arrived in Montreal from New York, Philadelphia, Boston, and other American cities, thinking that in Canada it might be easier to find work. Meanwhile, Jewish immigrants left Montreal for American cities, hoping to escape the crisis. Relatives sought out relatives, an unemployed worker from one city went to a friend who still had a job.

Some immigrant workers moved to the country to become peddlers in the hope that among the farmers they would be shielded from the crisis. In those days every penny helped. A nickel went a long way, ten cents bought a full meal, and one could live on fifteen cents a day. Indeed, those who became peddlers or started small businesses did evade the crisis to some extent. Many who became country peddlers eventually became successful businessmen.

Others could not escape the economic depression. They were forced to turn to the soup kitchens. Many elderly gentlemen, who today own their own homes and have well-to-do sons and sons-in-law, will perhaps recall that during this depression they ate in soup kitchens because they did not have a dime to buy a meal.

Group of Jewish immigrant women, Toronto, 1910.
Montreal immigrants tried to escape the economic depression of
1907-08 by moving to Toronto and other cities. For these same
reasons Jewish immigrants came to Montreal.
Archives of Ontario F1405-23-081, MSR687 #7

Mass Meetings

IN THE YEARS OF IMMIGRATION, when most Jews were workers, peddlers, and small businessmen, economic problems played a prominent role in the life of the Jewish community. A strike was an event of immense importance to the entire population. Every striker was a hero or a martyr. A scab was treated with extreme contempt.

No one would speak to a scab and if he did, he had to answer for it. When a scab came to Dufferin Park or to the mountain, he sat alone on a bench. Even his *landslayt* would avoid him. The wife of a scab was also made to feel the community's scorn. When she entered the grocery store, the grocer did not reply to her "good morning." When she came to the butcher shop, the butcher pretended not to hear her say goodbye.

Economic disputes erupted not only between employers and employees. Often fights broke out between housewives and the bakers and butchers. Occasionally the bakers would decide to raise the price of bread. This was an event with dire consequences in the Jewish neighbourhood. A fierce struggle ensued. Similarly, a storm of protest was unleashed if the butchers decided to raise the price of meat.

The protests would begin in front of the shops, led by the tailors and cloakmakers. Small boys would appear handing out leaflets which called for action against the higher prices. The leaflets would invite everyone to a mass meeting at the Labour Temple or Prince Arthur Hall. Immigrants gladly attended these mass meetings which gave them an opportunity to hear community leaders and orators who were well-known in the Jewish milieu.

It was a pleasant experience for the immigrant to attend a meeting with many other Yiddish-speaking Jews in an atmosphere where he could feel at home. He was also profoundly impressed to see Jews speaking out freely, courageously, fearing no one.

The immigrant listened attentively to all the speakers at the mass meeting called in protest against the bakers who had raised the price of bread. The speeches seemed more and more interesting as the meeting progressed.

The first speaker, almost immediately after introducing the bread issue in Montreal, would turn his attention to the revolution against the czar in Russia. He would describe how Russian revolutionaries were fighting on the barricades in St. Petersburg and Odessa, in Riga and in Vilna, and would connect their struggle to the protest against the bakers in Montreal. He would quote from Karl Marx and Karl Kautsky to convince the crowd that it was necessary to conduct a campaign against the higher bread prices.

A second speaker had a slightly different revolutionary perspective. Instead of Karl Marx and Karl Kautsky, he would cite passages from Bakunin[87] and Kropotkin[88] and come to the conclusion that the bread problem would only be solved once the workers had founded their own cooperatives. Then the capitalists would automatically lose their power and the workers would become the bosses of the world.

Radicals were not the only speakers at the mass meetings. Non-socialists, such as community activists involved in sick benefit societies or smaller synagogues, also spoke. This type of speaker would present himself as a friend of the workers. In his introduction he would state that although he was not a socialist, nevertheless he identified with the poor. He would cite passages from the *Chumash* to show that the *Torah* commands support for the poor in their struggle against the rich. The immigrant Jews would listen to these quotations with great pleasure and spirited applause.

Then the speaker would tell a story by the Dubner Magid[89] or by other *maggidim*, who were known to the immigrants from the old country. The tales of the *maggidim* had a profound effect even on the radical speakers, who applauded the morals of these stories. To make his speech even more appealing, the speaker would weave in a few of Hershele Ostropoler's[90] jokes. The audience responded warmly to these jokes, and the hall shook with laughter. Then the speaker reminded himself of the grave issue at hand: what to do about the bakers who had raised the price of bread. The laughter in the hall ceased. Everyone became serious again. The speaker made a practical suggestion: the women should bake their own bread as they had done in the *shtetl*. This suggestion was met with enthusiastic applause.

The next speaker, also a non-socialist, spoke of unity. He pointed out that all the problems facing the Jews stemmed from their lack of solidarity. If all the Jews in the world were united, he shouted, the bakers would not dare to raise the price of bread.

This speaker recounted how Jews suffered the world over from a lack of unity. Beginning with Adam, he told how the quarrel between his two sons, Cain and Abel, resulted in the first tragic murder. Next he turned to Joseph and his brothers, dramatically describing how the brothers, ruled by hatred and envy, sold Joseph to the Ishmaelites. Then he spoke of the split between radicals and ordinary Jews in Montreal and concluded that to achieve a victory in their campaign against the bakers, Jews would have to be united and strive for solidarity among the Jewish people.

An oration of this kind drew loud applause. The immigrants were deeply moved to hear ordinary Jews talking about Bible stories, unity, and mutual support. After such a speech everyone would decide unanimously to declare a boycott against the bakers. Under no circumstances was anyone to buy bread for higher prices. Sometimes a boycott would end in a victory for the customers. At other times, the bakers prevailed.

View of Cartier Monument from Mount Royal, 1915.
"A scab was treated with extreme contempt ... When a scab came to the mountain, he sat alone on a bench."
Archives of Ontario C7-3, No. 11838

The *Keneder Adler* (The Jewish Daily Eagle)[91]

A MASSIVE WAVE of Jewish immigration to Canada began in 1905 and 1906. Each ship arriving from Europe brought large numbers of Jewish immigrants, both young and old. Children came to be reunited with their parents, parents came to children, wives to husbands, brides to their betrothed.

Although immigrants arrived from every country, most came from the Russian Empire. Immigration from Russia escalated because of the war with Japan and heightened anti-Semitism which manifested itself in pogroms against Jews in a number of cities and towns in Byelorussia, the Ukraine, and Bessarabia. The worst pogrom occurred in Kishinev. Intense hostility toward the czarist regime following the Kishinev pogrom resulted in an exodus of Jews from Russia of unprecedented proportions.

Scattered among the immigrants in ever increasing numbers were members of the intelligentsia, people who were passionately devoted to social activism. Some were former students in yeshivas and secondary schools (*gymnasia*), young men and women steeped in the culture and traditions of the old country who had already read Sholem Aleichem and Peretz, Reisen[92] and Nomberg,[93] Asch[94] and Pinski[95]—the modern Jewish writers of the day.

There were young and middle-aged people who were knowledgeable about contemporary Jewish politics, the ideas of Chibat Zion and the Haskalah, and the writings of Dr. Herzl,[96] Nordau,[97] Zangwill,[98] Achad Ha'am,[99] Sokolov[100] and Klausner.[101] In addition to Yiddish newspapers like *Fraynt*[102] and *Haynt*,[103] they also read *Hatsfirah*[104] and the liberal Russian newspapers *Rech'* and *Birzhevie Vedomosti*, and closely followed the dramatic struggle of the Russian liberals in the first State Duma of 1905 for equal rights and outside the Duma against the anti-Semitic St. Petersburg newspaper *Novoye Vremya*, the Black Hundreds,[105] Purishkevich[106] and Krushevan.[107]

In the first month or two after their arrival, these immigrants were quiet and reserved. After getting their bearings, they ventured out into the community, attended the various synagogues, organizations, and societies, and became active in one or more of these social venues.

The newcomers hailed from various countries and from a variety of cultural influences and backgrounds. They all sought their own social environment and cultural milieu. This was how Jewish Montreal became divided up into groups of diverse cultural orientations and tendencies. The two major orientations were uptown and downtown.

The uptowners were wealthy Jews who had long ago adapted to Canada both linguistically and intellectually and were only remotely concerned with the problems and aspirations of world Jewry. Downtowners, on the other hand, included poor and middle-class Jews, as well as a few affluent ones, who took an active interest in the problems of Jews all over the world. Their lives were infused with the culture and traditions of Eastern Europe. Their approach to philanthropy differed as well in that they were more sentimental and had more contact with the recipients of their charity.

As more immigrants arrived in Montreal, the demarcation between uptown and downtown became sharper. Downtown Jews began to found various philanthropic and social institutions completely independently of the uptowners. They also began to create Jewish cultural institutions establishing intellectual and cultural links between the Jewish community of Montreal and Jewish communities in other countries.

As the downtown Jewish community expanded, the need for a Yiddish newspaper became apparent. A group of downtown Jews began planning for a daily Yiddish paper, although the main initiative came from H. Wolofsky,[108] who was then the owner of a store that supplied merchandise to peddlers. Of course it was not an easy plan to execute, but in 1907 their goal was achieved. In that year the *Keneder Adler* began publication in Montreal.

The launching of the *Adler* was a momentous occasion for the Jews of Montreal and rest of Canadian Jewry. At the outset there was uncertainty regarding its viability. Many Montreal Jews at the time believed that it was a risky undertaking as the population was too small to sustain a daily newspaper. But the newspaper survived and proved invaluable in the formation of national cultural institutions and expanding the scope of organized Jewish life in Montreal.

In the first year or two after the appearance of the *Keneder Adler*, a number of community organizations and societies for charitable and other purposes were founded in Montreal. Organizations established earlier were revitalized thanks to the newspaper. For the Jews arriving from Europe after 1907 it was gratifying to find that they had landed in a city with a Yiddish daily newspaper. They felt less isolated and alone during their initial period of adjustment, and within the Jewish community they did not feel so green. This counted for a great deal.

From the *Keneder Adler* Jewish immigrants learned many facts about Canada of which they were previously ignorant. They began to be aware of Jews in other Canadian communities such as Ottawa, Toronto, and Winnipeg. They were informed of prominent Jews in Canadian cities other than Montreal. The *Keneder Adler* became central in Jewish communal life and the mouthpiece for the young Jewish community of Canada.

The first issue of the Yiddish version of the *Keneder Adler*,
August 30, 1907.

Canada

WHEN THE *Keneder Adler* began publication in 1907 Jewish problems were minor compared to those in the aftermath of World War II. At that time Jewish newspapers carried articles on Zionism and anti-Semitism but their frame of reference was much more limited.

Before the appearance of the *Keneder Adler*, immigrant Jews read newspapers from New York which printed nothing about Canada. Newspapers from the old country also contained little information about Canada except for the fact that it was a faraway land. Consequently the early immigrants knew very little about Canada.

The *Keneder Adler* served as their window to the land and its people. They discovered that they had settled in a vast county, one of the largest in the world, and that the country was divided into provinces just as Russia was divided into *guberniias*. Each province had a premier just as each *guberniia* had a governor. They learned there were other large cities in Canada where Jews lived besides Montreal such as Toronto, Ottawa, Hamilton, Halifax, and Winnipeg. And they also became aware that somewhere far, far away, even further than Winnipeg, there were Jewish agricultural colonies settled exclusively by Jewish farmers and subsidized by the ICA, the Jewish Colonization Association, an organization which received much attention in the Eastern European newspapers *Fraynt*, *Haynt*, and *Hatsfirah*.[109]

They read about regions of Canada where coal and gold were mined and that in the provinces west of Winnipeg enough wheat and corn were grown to feed almost half the population of the world.

They learned that Jews were to be found in the farthest reaches of the country who had come from many different lands such as Russia, Rumania, Galicia, Bukovina, and Hungary. Many of these immigrant Jews, after traveling the length and breadth of the country, had settled in small towns without tailoring shops or cloak shops where they became fully Canadianized and economically successful even more quickly than the immigrants who had come to Montreal, the great metropolis.

Canada, they discovered, was so immense that to traverse it by train from sea to sea required several days. In Canada all citizens could freely choose any occupation they wanted. Every kind of business and industry existed here where one could find employment, as well as universities where young people who wished to study could graduate as doctors, lawyers, engineers, and so on.

Through the *Keneder Adler* immigrant Jews became acquainted with the government of the country. The newspaper frequently carried stories about the Prime Minister, Sir Wilfrid Laurier, and his cabinet ministers who governed the country from Ottawa, the capital. The immigrants were extremely impressed by the highly complimentary newspaper articles about Prime Minister Laurier who was portrayed as an *oyev-yisroel*, a friend of the Jewish people, and one of the greatest liberals in the world.

The *Keneder Adler* recounted how Prime Minister Laurier took a keen interest in the plight of the Jews of Russia and Rumania. He was said to have great sympathy for the Rumanian *fusgeyers* who traveled by foot to Hamburg and then on to America in protest against their government which encouraged anti-Semitic attacks on Jews. It was reported that Prime Minister Laurier was deeply troubled by the pogroms perpetrated against the Russian Jews living under the czarist regime. On one occasion he had spoken with tears in his eyes in the Ottawa synagogue at a mass meeting convened to protest the Kishinev pogrom.

Russian and Rumanian Jews immediately felt profound respect for the Canadian Prime Minister who openly condemned anti-Semitism in their countries of origin. They regarded him as one of the *khside-umes-ho'oylem*, the gentile friends of the Jews. The Jews of Bukovina and Galicia likened him to Franz Joseph whom they also regarded as an *oyev-yisroel*, and a great liberal. When Franz Joseph would visit a small *shtetl* in Galicia, or so the Jews of Galicia said, Christians would greet him with their religious objects and the Jews with a Torah scroll. Franz Joseph would first approach the Jewish delegation, kiss the Torah and only afterward turn to the Christians to kiss their holy objects.

Articles about Laurier's cabinet ministers also appeared frequently in the *Keneder Adler*. They were portrayed as friendly people but, more significantly, as liberals. The word "liberal" was very dear to the hearts of the Jewish immigrants of Russia and Rumania. In Russia it was the liberals who were demanding the abolition of the Pale of Settlement and equal rights for the Jews. The Russian Jews compared the Liberal cabinet ministers in Canada to such Russian liberals as Miliukov,[110] Maklakov,[111] and Roditchev,[112] who defended the Jews in the Russian Duma. They were happy to have settled in a country with a Liberal government and thanked God that they were free of the czar's regime with its anti-Semitic ministers and governors.

Zelda and Solomon Marshall with daughter Ida,
Sydney Mines, Nova Scotia, 1905.
Immigrant Jews settled in small towns across Canada.
Zelda and Solomon Marshall (uncle of Israel Medres)
opened a general store in Sydney Mines.
Courtesy of Abie and Zelda Marshall.

78

The City

WITH THE ADVENT of the *Keneder Adler*, immigrant Jews were able to become more familiar with the city. Before the newspaper was available, their knowledge of Montreal was limited to a few streets. They were well acquainted with the streets where they lived, worked, and went for walks such as Main, St. Catherine, Notre Dame, and Craig. They knew about Dorchester Street because of the Montreal General Hospital and De la Commune Street where they boarded the boat to St. Helen's Island. But the city in general was strange and unfamiliar.

Before the publication of the *Keneder Adler*, Jewish immigrants had only read the newspapers from New York. They were informed of everything that was going on there. They knew the names of all the streets in New York's East Side—streets where the pushcart peddlers stood, streets which were always in darkness because elevated trains ran above them, streets where the old tenement buildings were located. All this was described in the articles and stories which they read in the Yiddish newspapers from New York. Yet they knew very little about the streets of Montreal.

Similarly, Montreal Jews learned about every major fire in New York. When a New York policeman arrested a pushcart peddler on the East Side for peddling without a license, it was known in Montreal the very next day and Jewish immigrants discussed it as a noteworthy event. They knew the names of New York's gangsters and gamblers, and whenever two gangsters fought each other on the East Side, it was an important news item brought to the immigrant Jews of Montreal by the New York papers.

New immigrants who could not read the English newspapers were ignorant of what was happening in their city. For them Montreal was a closed book. The *Keneder Adler* opened that book for them. It revealed to them that they lived in a large metropolis with people of diverse languages, races, beliefs, and cultures.

They learned that although Montreal was not the capital of the country nor even of the province, it was the largest city in Canada and one of the largest in North America, with distinguished universities and important industries. World famous artists, first class singers, and musicians whose names they had already heard in Europe, often visited Montreal.

Reading the *Keneder Adler* gave them the opportunity to become acquainted with the inhabitants of the city. They discovered that here in Montreal besides workers and bosses, foremen and designers, peddlers and grocers, there were lawyers and judges, a city mayor and aldermen, elected members of the Quebec Legislative Assembly and members of the federal Parliament in Ottawa.

There were also people who wrote in English and French. Most of the writers were well-disposed toward Jews and immigrants, but some were hostile to the Jews and to Jewish immigration from Russia and Rumania. They tried to find fault with the immigrants. The *Keneder Adler* responded to these writers who mainly wrote for small French-language newspapers or magazines.

There are all kinds of fish in the sea and, in a big city, all kinds of people. And Jewish immigrants learned from the *Keneder Adler* that among the people of Montreal there were hoodlums who once in a while would physically assault Jews. It was painful for the immigrant Jews from Russia and Rumania to hear that in Montreal Jews had to contend with these ruffians. Yet they found consolation in the knowledge that the hoodlums were only a small minority of the population and that if one were capable of hitting them back in self-defence, one could do so.

They were also introduced to an organization for Jews, a committee of sorts which was especially set up to protect Jews from these bullies. This organization, which was called the Citizens' League, was dedicated to helping immigrant Jews obtain Canadian citizenship.

The *Keneder Adler* made the immigrants aware of the similarities between Montreal and New York. There were gangsters and gamblers in Montreal, and at times dangerous criminals were brought to trial in Montreal's courtrooms. Occasionally people stood trial for murder. Sometimes the murder was committed during a robbery, sometimes in the course of an illicit love affair, sometimes for revenge or for some other motive.

Thanks to the newspaper Jewish immigrants became well-informed about the city, its attractive aspects as well as its seamy side.

The Community

IN THE YEAR that the *Keneder Adler* commenced publication, there was an economic depression in the country causing severe suffering among the immigrant Jews. Many lost their jobs, while those who continued to be employed earned very little. The downtown Jews began to establish charitable organizations to assist families in straitened circumstances.

The *Malbish Arumim* Society was founded to provide clothing to children of poor families. Hundreds of working class parents, including tailors who made clothes for others, could not afford to clothe their own children who were pupils at Dufferin School or Aberdeen School.

The Hebrew Consumptive Aid Society was created to assist the families of tailors and cloakmakers when a member of the family fell ill with tuberculosis. In those days, workers in the needle trades spent ten hours a day in the sweatshops and even longer during the busy season. Tailors were typically pale and thin, and many suffered from tuberculosis. The Ladies' Relief Society, founded by women to discretely assist families who wished to conceal their poverty, was among the several charitable organizations set up at this time.

The *Keneder Adler* was instrumental in the development of organized Jewish community life by providing a network among the various Jewish groups. This period also saw the founding of fraternal organizations. For example, in 1907 the Bessarabian Jews formed the Bessarabian Hebrew Sick Benefit Society and in the same year a branch of the *Arbeiter Ring* was created in Montreal. The few organizations in existence prior to this time were revitalized.

Orthodox Jews, including Hasidim, also became active in founding new congregations. Among the older immigrants brought here by their children were Hasidim, who, in the small towns of Eastern Europe, were followers of Hasidic rabbis and had prayed in small Hasidic synagogues. In their first years in Montreal they missed these small synagogues and their Hasidic style of prayer. Once they began to adjust to the new environment and realized that it was not difficult to set up a congregation, they banded together to found small synagogues where the atmosphere and style of prayer more or less resembled the Hasidic synagogues of Eastern Europe.

Several *misnagdim*, non-Hasidic Orthodox Jews, also established small synagogues. They, too, sought a more religious atmosphere than that of the larger synagogues as well as a place they could attend more often. They enjoyed going to synagogue on a daily basis to tell stories and anecdotes about the great rabbis of the past such as Rabbi Isaac Elhanan,[113] Rabbi Chaim Brisker,[114] and Rav Israel Meir Radiner, the Chafetz Chaim.[115]

The cultural sphere also showed signs of growth and enrichment. In the Jewish bookstores on Main Street more serious books began to make their appearance, including books on history and science. For ten or fifteen cents one could buy a small booklet about chemistry, astronomy, or the wireless telegraph. Although hard-working new immigrants generally had no time to read books, just before Passover or Sukkoth, the Feast of Tabernacles, they would purchase the *Minikes' yon-tev bleter*,[116] where almost all the Jewish writers and community leaders in America were represented by articles, stories, and poems. The average immigrant who bought the *Minikes yon-tev bleter* prior to Passover, had enough reading material for the entire summer, right up to Sukkoth. The *bleter* he purchased before Sukkoth would last him all winter long until it was time for Passover again.

Although the majority of immigrants had no time for books, every immigrant read the newspaper. Even those who had never read newspapers in the old country read Yiddish newspapers on this side of the ocean. As a result, the newspapers in the United States and Canada had to be simplified and easy to read to accommodate this kind of reader which the Yiddish and Hebrew newspapers in Russia never had.

When the *Keneder Adler* went into circulation, the Yiddish and Hebrew newspapers dealt with the following issues which were the most pressing problems facing the Jews of that era: What was to become of the Jews of Russia? Would the liberal and cultural ideas of Western Europe influence the czarist regime to repeal the discriminatory laws against the Jews or not?

Many Jewish writers were optimistic. In their enthusiasm over the cultured and liberal-minded people of Western Europe, they were convinced that pressure from London and Paris would persuade the czar to give Russian Jews equal rights. Other writers were pessimists. They had no faith in the diplomats and statesmen from London and Paris who were interested in supporting the czar because English and French capitalists were investing a great deal of money in Russian industries and enterprises. Only a revolution from within, they wrote, would bring equality for Jews.

There was also the question of Palestine. Would the Turkish government give the Zionists a charter over the Land of Israel? The optimists believed that civilized European countries would welcome the Young Turks marking the beginning of a bright new era for all mankind, including the Jews. The pessimists predicted that the great European powers would plot against the new Turkey and incite smaller countries to go to war in order to destroy the Turkish Empire.

In those days the Jewish newspapers were full of news about the Young Turks, Abdul Hamid,[117] the Balkans, Tripoli, and the Dardenelles—especially the Dardenelles. In its first few years of publication, the leading news stories in the *Keneder Adler* dealt with the campaigns which Italy, and then the Balkan States, conducted against Turkey.

The Goldberg family, Kielce, Poland. The Jewish community in Montreal was preoccupied with the fate of Jews in the Russian Empire, which until its demise, included much of Poland.
Courtesy of Dr. Shim Felsen.

Writers

VERY FEW YIDDISH writers lived in Montreal when the *Keneder Adler* went into circulation. In fact, no one was even aware of their existence. The first two editors had to be imported from New York, which already had a large community of writers and poets.

The first editor was Michael Aronson,[118] who, after a short time returned to New York. Next came A. Wohliner (Louis Landau)[119] who was already a prominent journalist and public affairs columnist. He, too, did not remain with the paper for long and was succeeded by A. A. Roback,[120] a young Montrealer whose brief tenure was followed by another editor from New York, Dr. Wortsman.[121] The first important editor of the newspaper was Reuben Brainin who came to Montreal in 1912 when the paper was five years old.

The first Montrealer to write for the newspaper was B. G. Sack.[122] In contrast to his brother, Mendel Leib Sack, who enjoyed a reputation as a Hebraist, pedagogue, and scholar as well as a community leader, B.G. Sack was completely unknown in Montreal. When B.G. Sack heard that a daily newspaper was about to be published, he submitted an article which was well received. Thus a local writer was discovered and the *Keneder Adler* had its first staff writer. B. G. Sack began his career with the *Keneder Adler,* and the *Keneder Adler* began with him. Editors changed, writers came and went, but not Sack. He has been with the newspaper from its inception until today as a public affairs columnist, editorial writer, and historian of Jewish life in Canada.

Other local writers emerged over the next few years. They were recruited from among those readers with intellectual and literary interests. One was Shmuel Talpis,[123] a businessman known for his expertise in Jewish law and lore. Another was the student A. A. Roback, already mentioned, who graduated from McGill University and became an eminent scientist, an author of books about psychology, and an expert in modern Yiddish literature. Other writers were I. Yampolsky,[124] Moishe Shmuelson,[125] S. Shneur,[126] Kornblitt,[127] and Joel Leib Malamut.[128]

Almost all the Yiddish writers in those days became writers because they were intelligent readers. Before emigrating from the old country they had read scores of books and journals in Hebrew, Russian, and other languages. Once in America they became involved in community activities and felt compelled to write. Former yeshiva students began writing novels which were greeted by their readers with tremendous enthusiasm. Talmudists from the yeshivas of Volozhin,[129] Telz,[130] Slobodka,[131] and Mir,[132] experts in *pilpul* (subtle argumentation) and *Gemara*, began to write hair-splitting articles on socialist theory and philosophy, on which proletarian intellectuals with radical inclinations sharpened their wits.

Among the intellectual immigrants were former university students from Russia or Rumania who began to write about moral issues such as relations between brides and grooms, husbands and wives, parents and children. Former Hebraist *maskilim* became specialists in literary criticism, cultural studies, or plays for the theatre. Intellectual factory workers who had received their education through party proclamations began to write short stories or poetry.

The staff of the *Keneder Adler*, 1927, including B.G. Sack seated second from left next to H. Wolofsky and I. Rabinovitch. Philip Wolofsky, L. Chafetz, and I. Medres are standing at the back.

The Press

Montreal Jews read the New York papers before the *Keneder Adler* was available and have continued to do so to this very day. With regard to Jewish issues, the New York papers had a tremendous impact on the Jews of Canada.

Thanks to these newspapers, new immigrants became familiar with the leaders of the American Jewish community. The newspapers frequently carried stories about Jacob Schiff, an eminent Wall Street banker who was also a great philanthropist. Another important philanthropist often written about was Nathan Strauss.[133] Much space was devoted to the two famous lawyers and community leaders Louis Marshall[134] and Samuel Intermayer.[135] Louis Marshall was considered one of the greatest defenders of Jewish rights of his time.

Within the Zionist movement were such luminaries as Jacob de Haas,[136] Louis Lipsky,[137] Louis Brandeis,[138] Joseph Barandes,[139] and Abe Goldberg.[140] Pre-eminent among the Labour Zionists were Dr. N. Syrkin[141] and Dr. Chaim Zhitlovsky.[142] Most famous in working class and socialist circles were Morris Hillquit,[143] Meir London,[144] Schlesinger,[145] Shiplacoff,[146] and Max Pine.[147]

Professor Getzel Zelikowitch[148] was among the popular writers in the *Tageblatt*[149]. He wrote about Jewish religion and scholarship as well as high-level politics. In all his articles he quoted passages from the Gemara and verses from the Chumash.

Those Jews who had no patience for world politics or Jewish philosophy enjoyed the fiction of M. Seifert.[150] The protagonists of his novels were simple, uneducated Jews with warm Jewish hearts and noble souls who adjusted well to the new world, America.

Many found pleasure in reading Tashrak's[151] humorous stories in the *Tageblatt*. Everyone was interested in Chaim, the custom-peddler, one of Tashrak's Jewish immigrant types who was in the process of adapting to life in America.

The Jews who read the *Varheit*[152] delighted in Louis Miller's dynamic editorials in which he would constantly rant and rave. He was always fighting on behalf of the Jewish people or in the name of the oppressed masses. He attacked both the left and the right. Sometimes in his editorials he would passionately denounce the industrial and railway magnates for organizing trusts and oppressing the workers and the poor of America. He castigated the Wall Street barons for lending money to the governments of Russia and Rumania which persecuted their Jewish inhabitants. Occasionally he would rail against the President of the United States in an attempt to convince him to break off diplomatic relations with Russia because the czar refused to repeal the discriminatory laws against Jews. At other times he directed his fury at the Reform rabbis for rewriting the *siddur*, the daily prayer book, or for being either indifferent or negative to Jewish national issues, especially Zionism. He also criticized the orthodox rabbis for not wanting to reform Jewish law by doing away with certain customs like the *khalitse*.[153]

Another popular writer for the *Varheit* was D. M. Hermolin who taught the immigrant Jews about American morals, ethics, customs, and etiquette. He wrote editorials on how to achieve success as Jews and as citizens in America. In his articles he would quote sentences from the Chumash, commentaries from the Talmud, and the fables of famous *maggidim*. He also cited Greek philosophers, Russian classicists, French romantics, German militarists, Chinese thinkers, English statesmen, and American presidents.

The *Forward* printed articles about revolutionary socialists, lengthy strikes, radical organizations, the Industrial Workers of the World, Bill Haywood, and Eugene Debs. Freethinkers and heretics relished B. Feigenbaum's[154] anti-religious articles. Orthodox Jews feared Feigenbaum because he would quote from the Talmud and the Chumash in his diatribes against religion.

Traditional Judaism and Zionism were subject to hostile attacks in the *Forward*. Other writers besides Feigenbaum targeted orthodox Judaism. Even the editor, Abe Kahan,[155] tackled this subject, especially on the eve of Rosh Hashana or Passover. Just before Passover topics like socialism, the *seder*, the *Haggadah*, and *kneydlakh* dominated the *Forward*. The basic question was: Could a committed socialist take his seat at the *seder* to please his religious parents? The response was far from unanimous. Socialist writers were divided in their opinions. The editor himself was rather liberal. He went so far as to permit the eating of *kneydlakh*, but no more.

Many readers of the *Forward* had neither the patience nor the ability to read weighty theoretical articles on socialism and internationalism. For them there was light reading such as the exciting novels of Leon Gottlieb, the short stories of Z. Libin,[156] and the *Bintel Brief* ("Bundle of Letters") which dealt on a daily basis with the problems of family life, jealousy, love, and treachery. Sometimes there was even a debate over free love.

And this, more or less, is how the Yiddish press appeared in the days when a large number of Jews in Canada and the United States had not yet become acculturated.

Montreal Jews read New York papers like the *Forward* before the *Keneder Adler* was available and continued to do so.

Boarders

THOSE IMMIGRANTS who earned a good living and were able to save did not have long to wait before they could purchase steamship tickets for their families in Europe. Within a short time they were able to stop living as boarders and settle into lodgings of their own.

Other immigrants earned little. For the first few months, while learning a new trade, they worked at half pay, barely enough to sustain themselves. Therefore it took longer before they could send for their wives and children. There were immigrants who remained boarders for two or three years renting rooms from strangers.

The matter of steamship passage was crucial in those days. The steamship ticket offices were prominent institutions in the Jewish community.[157] They were like information bureaus for all matters relating to immigrant Jews. The steamship agent possessed a great deal of information needed by the Jewish immigrants. They trusted him and sought his advice as from a brother about their families in Europe, whether to bring them now when they were barely settled, or to wait a few months to become more established, save some money, or be more secure in their jobs.

The ticket agent would strongly urge the immigrants to book passage for their families right away. He would inform them of the following basic facts. First, it was important for the children to arrive as soon as possible to begin school in order to become fully Canadianized, to go to high school and eventually university where they could study medicine or law. Secondly, he advised immigrants not to be afraid that they were not yet established. This was not the old country . . . they would make a living. Thirdly, when their wives arrived they could rent a larger flat with five or six rooms, take in boarders and then everything would be "all right."

The "boarder" phenomenon had a profound impact on Jewish life which was reflected in the press, in literature, and in the theatre. The newspapers would print many sketches and stories in which the protagonists were male or female boarders. The same was true of a large number of the melodramas in the Yiddish theatre. A typical plot went like this. A female boarder enters a happy Jewish home. She works as a finisher in a cloakshop or a baster in a tailor shop. Although she has a fiancé in the old country, she nevertheless falls in love with the husband and turns his head. He abandons his family and runs off with the boarder to another city.

In another melodrama the plot is reversed. A male boarder enters a family's happy home. He is handsome, elegant, smokes cigarettes, sports a gold tooth, tells jokes, and sings rhyming couplets from the Yiddish theatre. The wife falls in love with him, leaves her husband and children, including a sick baby, and runs away with the boarder to Canada.

While a boarder running off with a wife or a husband was a common occurrence in the plays of the Yiddish theatre, occasionally it happened in real life. When it did, a search was begun at once for the missing husband. Finding him was not a difficult task. The *Forward* would run his picture in its Gallery of Missing Husbands, which in those days was an important feature of the newspaper. The photographs in the Gallery were closely scrutinized, and in the process Jewish immigrants often recognized someone they had known in Eastern Europe. In most cases they would recall that even in the old country that person was a scoundrel, a swindler, and a cheat. Everyone who studied the Gallery took a keen interest in identifying these people to ensure that they fell into the proper hands and received the punishment they deserved.

In Montreal this rogues' gallery was studied assiduously because many of the missing people would hide in Canada. Sometimes a husband who had deserted his family for another woman or for some other reason was recognized. When the identification was made, there was a great deal of excitement. The person could be a factory worker, a small businessman, a salesman, or a clerk in a store. Mr. Kaplansky of the Legal Aid Department at the Baron de Hirsch Institute, who was in charge of such matters, was notified at once. Acting on this information, he took immediate steps to contact the alleged culprit. Sometimes it turned out to be a case of mistaken identity, where the man had no connection to the person whose picture appeared in the Gallery of Missing Husbands.

Occasionally, however, the identification was accurate, causing a sensation in the Jewish community. The news spread to all the sweatshops in the city. Everyone talked about the man who had been recognized from the Gallery, about how respectable, decent, and honourable he appeared to people who had known him. No one would have suspected him of abandoning a wife and children for another woman.

The man, of course, was quickly arrested and sent back to the city whence he had come.

Sophie Victor Medres and a cousin.
Sophie Medres arrived in Montreal alone in 1908 at the age
of seventeen. She worked in a clothing factory, saving enough to
bring over her parents, two younger brothers, and a sister
from Lithuania.

The Monument National

MONTREAL WAS ALWAYS an important centre for Yiddish theatre. There were years when Yiddish productions were mounted every night of the week. All the stars of the American Yiddish theatre performed at the Monument National Theatre on Main Street near Dorchester. All the plays written for the Yiddish stage from dramas to comedies were presented there. Not one reputable actor or actress and not a single important Yiddish play failed to appear in Montreal. Even though Yiddish plays were staged in other buildings such as the one on La Gauchetière Street near Main, or the large theatre on St. Catherine near St. Dominique, or a building on Main Street near Prince Arthur, the main theatre of Jewish Montreal was the Monument National Theatre.[158]

The Monument National Theatre was located in the very heart of the Jewish neighbourhood. Large political demonstrations on behalf of Jewish causes were also held there. On Rosh Hashana and Yom Kippur it became a synagogue, but unlike any synagogue the immigrants had seen in Eastern Europe. It was a private synagogue arranged especially for the High Holidays by the theatre manager in charge of the Yiddish productions, Mr. Mitnick.[159]

In those days the Jewish masses were more interested in Yiddish theatre than they are today. The theatre provided them with entertainment, education, and a social life. Modern movies did not yet exist; no one had heard of Hollywood. There was no better entertainment than the Yiddish theatre.

In the theatre the Jewish immigrants learned about morals and manners. Many plays ended with a lesson on how to live and conduct oneself with other people. In addition, one could learn from the actors and actresses how to speak, walk, sit, bow, sing, tell a joke, and be romantic.

For immigrants, an outing to the Yiddish theatre was a festive occasion. They would dress in their finest clothes as for a wedding. People who frequented the theatre on a regular basis were those who earned more money, those who had arrived. It was easy to recognize these successful people. The surest sign that they had been in the country for a long time, perhaps as long as ten years, was their gold teeth. A well-to-do husband would wear one or two massive gold rings and a gold watch and chain over his vest. His wife, in an oversized hat with a long feather, was adorned with jewelry, much of it from the old country. The gold teeth, however, were most certainly acquired here in Canada.

The plays of the Yiddish theatre taught the immigrants ethics and history. Many plays ended with the lesson that one must be honourable, that one must not chase after money, or get involved with strange women, or gamble, or make friends with people of bad character. In many plays with historical themes, the main characters were either biblical heroes or figures from the past.

Immigrant Jews, who during their childhood in the old country had never had the opportunity to study even the most elementary subjects, were able to learn about Jewish historical events by attending the theatre. For example, when they saw Goldfaden's[160] *Bar Kochba* or *Shulamis*, they became acquainted with fascinating and romantic chapters in Jewish history which gave them not only visual enjoyment but intellectual stimulation.

They learned to sing from Goldfaden's operas. The songs in his operettas were sung in every Jewish home, and the songs from *Bar Kochba* were sung at Zionist meetings and conferences. The historical Bar Kochba was the most popular Zionist propagandist among the Jewish masses in those days.

However, Goldfaden's historical works could not be produced very often at the Monument National. To stage one of his operas required a chorus of singers and a large cast. The plays of Lateiner[161] were performed more frequently because they were much simpler, although they, too, contained historical motifs. Lateiner wrote plays and operettas about King David and his son, King Solomon. His operetta, *The Love of Zion* , his plays, *The Destruction of Jerusalem* and *The Emperor Nero,* were all works which portrayed Jewish life in ancient Israel.

Such dramas as *Alexander the Prince of Jerusalem* or *Ezra the Eternal Jew* or *Daniel in the Lion's Den* also enriched the historical knowledge of the immigrants. Equally popular were Lateiner's many non-historical plays such as *Khinke-Pinke, Love and Passion, Blood Wedding, Truth and Falsehood.*

The immigrants learned a great deal from other dramas and melodramas. The dramas of Jacob Gordin[162] were the subject of much controversy in the Yiddish press. From time to time Jewish writers would conduct a war of words over one of his plays. For example, if the *Varheit* praised it, the *Forward* would do the opposite. The more the newspapers fought over a play, the larger the audience became, as people went to see what the fuss was all about. The best Jewish actors and actresses appeared in Gordin's plays.

Even those who had never seen him, knew what Gordin looked like from pictures in the Yiddish newspapers. His appearance was greatly respected. He wore a black beard like Dr. Herzl's, and it was reported that besides being a playwright, he was also a socialist. Nevertheless the socialist newspaper, the *Forward*, often gave him bad reviews. This attracted even more attention among the immigrant Jews who took an interest in the Yiddish theatre. He was considered a moralist and intellectual, and was compared to all the great playwrights of Russia, France, and other countries.

Although Jacob Gordin's dramas were often presented at the Monument National Theatre, he himself was never seen there. Other playwrights, however, did come to Montreal occasionally and were present at the Monument National when their plays were performed. Among those who were spotted in Montreal from time to time were David Pinski[163] and Peretz Hirshbein.[164] They would come in their later years to deliver a lecture or read from their work. Hirshbein, in addition to being a playwright, had his own theatre company with which he traveled from country to country and from city to city.

There were playwrights who were also known as novelists and short story writers. Among them were Pinski, Hirshbein, Z. Libin,[165] Leon Kobrin,[166] and Sholem Asch,[167] whose *God of Vengeance* played many times at the Monument National Theatre.

Sometimes the work of a Montreal playwright was performed at the Monument National. Such an event received a great deal of attention in the city. Everyone talked about it. It was not easy for the playwright to write a drama. He would work on it for a long time. Then, when the play was completed, he had the difficult task of convincing the theatre managers and theatrical troupes to hear him read his play. The manager and the actors would finally agree under intense pressure to hear the local playwright, and produce his play. They reasoned that perhaps Montreal Jews would attend in droves, filling every nook and cranny of the theatre, if they heard that the play being presented was written by one of their own, someone known to many of the tailors, cloakmakers, and grocers.

When the play was finally produced, a few new faces did indeed make their appearance in the Monument National. Tailors and cloakmakers acquainted with the playwright from the sweatshop, his *landslayt*, and neighbours would all attend. The playwright himself would naturally be on top of the world. He would sit in a box seat and everyone would look up at him with great admiration. Between the third and fourth acts he would be led onto the stage and presented to the public. Everyone was happy and a festive mood pervaded the theatre.

But Montreal playwrights did not write many plays. In most cases, one sufficed. The local playwright would resume his former occupation and the actors would return to their New York repertoire. Within a matter of weeks, the Montreal playwright was completely forgotten.

In the old days, actors who appeared in the Yiddish theatre were very popular with the Jewish masses. They had a privileged status in Jewish society. Among the famous stars were: Jacob Adler,[168] Zygmund Mogulesko,[169] David Kessler,[170] Boris Thomashefsky,[171] Kenni Liptzen,[172] Regina Prager,[173] and Bertha Kalish.[174] Even the immigrants who came from large cities and had attended the theatres in Warsaw, Vilna, Odessa, Lemberg, Lodz and Bucharest were excited about these stars. For immigrant Jews who had never seen Yiddish theatre in the old country, the Monument National was simply the paradise of the new world.

When Madame Liptzen played Mirele Efros[175] it was a momentous occasion. The theatre was packed. When Mirele cried, the women in the audience—and some of the men—would weep with her. Sometimes a woman from the audience would become so hysterical that she had to be led out of the theatre so that the entire audience would not break down.

After a performance of *Mirele Efros* many immigrants went home with the lesson that one should not be too good to one's children by giving them their inheritance during one's lifetime. They learned the same lesson when Jacob Adler played the part of King Lear. After the performance immigrants left the theatre in a trance, their eyes red from crying and their hearts broken over King Lear's tragic fate.

When David Kessler performed in Gordin's *Got, mentsch un tayvl* (God, Man and Devil) at the Monument National, there was excitement in the Jewish streets. The immigrants idolized Kessler, above all in his role as Hershele Dubrovner. For some time the three stars, Kessler, Adler, and

Kenni Liptzen, dominated the Yiddish stage in New York and the Monument National in Montreal.

The newcomer, who was not yet Canadianized, felt comfortable in the Yiddish theatre not only because of the performance, but because of the warm congeniality and Yiddish-speaking atmosphere he found there. He was inspired by the old country types portrayed on stage by the actors who reminded him of familiar and beloved people from Eastern Europe. His favorite actors and actresses, especially the stars, enchanted him with their Yiddish songs about homesickness and the holy Sabbath, about hatred toward the czar and the perpetrators of pogroms, the enemies of the Jewish people. There were songs that idealized the immigrant Jews themselves, portraying them as impoverished workers, honest toilers slaving away in free America.

Jacob Gordin (1853-1909).
The Gordin era was described as the Golden Age of Yiddish Theatre. The first Yiddish production presented in Montreal was Gordin's *The Jewish King Lear,* performed by Isaac Zolotarevsky's troupe at the Monument National Theatre in February 1897.
Courtesy of Beth Kaplan.

Art and Business

THEIR ATTRACTION to the dramatic arts brought Jewish actors to the Yiddish theatre. The business aspect, of course, also played an important role. In the heyday of the Yiddish theatre, when Adler, Kessler, Liptzen, and Jacob Gordin's dramas dominated the stage, there was no apparent conflict between art and business. Only later did the conflict come into sharp focus.

Even in the golden age of Adler, Kessler, and Liptzin there were smaller companies with actors of lesser talents who performed banal melodramas. Intellectuals referred to these melodramas as *shund* (trash). Yet these second-rate plays were popular with many people, especially women and girls whose tastes in art and literature were rather limited. Therefore, managers of large theatres became warmly disposed to these melodramas.

Talented artists also began to take an interest in the second-rate plays, taking into account the predilections of the audience. Mirele Efros, the great personage of the Yiddish stage, had to relinquish her privileged place to "the white slave." Almost every melodrama featured an evil, unscrupulous, immoral procurer—an "Alphonse." He would seduce an innocent girl who would find herself the unwed mother of an illegitimate child. Despised and shunned by society, she became a white slave.[176]

The audience was intensely interested in the tragic fate of the white slave. The talent of the actors was of little concern. What counted was whether or not society was right in its attitude toward the white slave. Debates ensued among the theatre-goers. The radicals condemned society, arguing that in a socialist society unwed mothers and illegitimate children would be treated as everyone else instead of being ostracized. Non-radicals did not condemn society but rather the villainous "Alphonse." They maintained that such scoundrels should be sent to Sing-Sing or the electric chair.

From these melodramas, girls and women came away with the lesson that a girl should not trust a young man if she did not know him well. If a young man were to declare his love she should not believe him, unless he gave her a diamond engagement ring. Even then she had to be vigilant until the time of the wedding. Before the wedding, she had to find out whether, in fact, he really was single. Perhaps he had a wife in another city. She needed to study the photographs in the Gallery of Missing Husbands[177] in the *Forward* to be certain that his picture had not appeared there.

The conflict between art and trash raged in the Yiddish theatre, and for a long time it was one of the most heated debates in the cultural life of the Jewish community.

In the Yiddish newspapers, writers and theatre critics took the side of art. But theatre managers, who were fans of the second-rate plays, had the upper hand. Their position, that business took precedence over art, prevailed.

Some of the critics became worn down in the struggle for art. Seeing that they could not convince the managers, they made peace with the second rate plays and even began to look for—and discover—positive aspects about which they could write with enthusiasm. Other theatre critics, who could not come to terms with the melodramas, abandoned the theatre field completely and used their pens for other matters.

The conflict between art and trash was also evident in the Montreal Yiddish theatre. The stark melodramas about white slaves began to find their way into the Monument National, resulting in increased business. The manager was extremely pleased.

The critics in the *Keneder Adler* attacked these melodramas and demanded literary plays with trained and talented actors. Occasionally the manager had to accede to the demands of the *Adler* and its circle of intellectuals. This circle came into existence when Reuben Brainin became editor. Leon Chazanovitch,[178] an important writer on current affairs who edited the *Folkszeitung,* was also living in Montreal at this time. A few writers who had arrived in Montreal in Brainin's day also belonged to this circle. They included L.M. Benjamin,[179] H. M. Caiserman,[180] who was at the time a prominent leader in national-radical circles and in the *Folkszeitung*, B. Goldstein,[181] and Dr. Yehuda Kaufman,[182] who is now one of the most important intellectuals in Israel, as well as some writers who were mentioned in earlier chapters.

This intellectual circle grew even wider. Israel Rabinovich,[183] who began his career in journalism as a theatre critic, arrived at the *Keneder Adler*. His reviews attacking the melodramas drew a great deal of serious attention.

The growing Montreal intelligentsia had tremendous influence so that theatre circles had to heed their opinions. From time to time the Monument National made concessions to the "better taste of the better audiences."

Once in a while, artists came to Montreal who were completely unprepared to make peace with the second-rate plays. Outstanding among them were Maurice Schwartz[184] and Jacob Ben Ami,[185] around whom had gathered a group of committed and talented artists. Whenever they came to Montreal, they were met by many friends and admirers.

Monument National Theatre.
Notman Photographic Archives.

The First Movies

IMMIGRANT JEWS loved the Yiddish theatre. However, as they could not afford to go to the theatre very often, they pursued other less costly leisure activities. They would go to the movies.[186]

They were able to go to the cinema on a weekly basis. It was inexpensive, not more than five cents, and one could stay as long as one wanted. On a wintry day the cinema was very warm in comparison to the flats in the poor neighbourhoods where the newcomers then lived. Those who earned more could afford to see a movie at least twice a week or more.

By going to a movie, the immigrant was not only enjoying himself, but also learning a great deal. He discovered the geography of the new world, its rivers, mountains, fields, and forests. He also learned its history, and got a glimpse of its first inhabitants—the Indians.

In those days almost every moving picture was about red-skinned Indians who rode around half-naked on horseback. Their chiefs wore bizarre headdresses fashioned entirely of feathers. These Indians made a strange impression on the newcomers. In Eastern Europe they had never heard of such people. Only the intellectuals, who had read the story of Christopher Columbus, had some vague notion about the Indians. Now they could be viewed in their natural environment. Watching these movies, the immigrants had the impression that they were being educated about an important chapter in American history.

The early moving pictures showed how civilization was brought to America by the massacre of its native inhabitants. Every movie included a battle between the Indians and the "white men." Every battle would end in total victory for the latter.

After the crowd had seen their fill of Indians, other kinds of movies were shown in which the heroes were cowboys. The cowboy movies were as exciting and intriguing to the newcomers as the movies about Indians, and taught them about the development of American society. For a long time, in many of the states, particularly in the West, law and order was unknown and social problems, as well as quarrels between individuals, were settled by the gun. Men would shoot each other over a girl. The situation went from bad to worse until the sheriffs gained control and established the rule of law and the authority of the courts.

There were also movies about the American Civil War between the southern and northern states, a war which had erupted over the principles of freedom and racial equality. For the immigrants, these movies were important lessons in American geography and American history.

Yiddish Vaudeville

AFTER THE JEWISH IMMIGRANTS had been exposed to countless movies about cowboys and Indians, it became necessary to create new attractions to entice them to the movie theatres on Main Street. A few of the cinema owners brought Yiddish vaudeville to their establishments.

The vaudeville theatres featured actors and actresses who were not suitable for the theatre companies which staged serious dramas or even second-rate plays. Their talents were too modest for the professional theatre but too great to waste in the tailor shops. They were just right for vaudeville.

Many recent immigrants received these actors warmly, applauding enthusiastically. These were immigrants who were not yet comfortably settled and could not yet afford the tickets at the Monument National.

The programme of a typical Yiddish vaudeville performance would have looked something like this. A well-dressed middle-aged Jewish gentleman, with a gold watch and chain over his vest, would come out on stage to sing a few Yiddish songs. His voice was cantorial—but hoarse. His material was of a very serious nature. He would begin with a song about "how the Jews are beaten and tormented" (*Vi men shlogt un men plogt yidn*). Almost weeping, he would sing about the Spanish Inquisition, the Kishenev pogrom, and the Dreyfus case in France. The audience would sigh and applaud. His next number had social content: "Do not brag about your money because you can easily lose it" (*Mit kayn gelt tor men nit shtoltsirn, vayl men kon es gikh farlirn*)[187] and the audience would sing along.

After that he would perform a popular folksong which everyone knew by heart, for example, "Come home, come home, Yisrolikl" (*Kum, kum, Yisrolikl aheym, aheym*).[188] The audience would respond with the words "to your own beautiful land" (*In dem sheynem land, in dayn*). Then he would sing, "Come quickly and don't worry about a thing," and the audience would follow with, "and be a nation like the others." Finally, the singer and the audience together would finish with "Yisrolikl, brother, come quickly home."

After a song like this the audience would break out in wild applause. The singer seemed moved. He would smile and at the same time wipe his eyes, as if overcome with emotion. Before he left the stage, he would tackle a song in Russian, such as, for example, "*Hey Dubinushka, dai ukhnyem.*" [189] Many in the audience who came from Russia would help out with "*Ey Zeliana, sama poidyot!*"

This serious and solemn singer was followed by another who was lighthearted and jovial. The second performer, a young man in sporty white trousers and a blue serge jacket, with a round straw hat on his head and a cane in his hand, was a dancer as well as a singer. He would sing while dancing or dance while singing, and was extremely popular with the girls and young women.

Besides singing and dancing, he also told salty jokes. He would begin with a couple of jokes, followed by a rather risqué tune about a wife and a boarder which he sang while dancing. His next number was entirely different in character. With a very solemn, even pious, air he would perform a sentimental religious song such as, "On Friday night every Jew is a king" (*Fraytik af der nakht iz yeder yid a meylekh*), or "Sabbath in a Jew's Home" (*Shabes koydesh baym yidele*). The crowd would join in when he sang these Sabbath songs and applaud energetically.

Finally an actress would appear on the stage. Although a middle-aged woman, from afar she looked like a young prima donna. Dressed in a black evening gown, with a gold watch on her bosom and a gold chain around her neck, she performed a few songs.

The singer would begin with a popular folksong familiar to all the immigrants from the old country. One of the most popular songs in those days was "A Letter to Mother" (A *brivele der mamen*).[190] Everyone wanted her to sing this song, and no sooner had she begun, than the audience would join in, "Do not tarry" (*Zolstu nit farzamen*). Then she and the audience together would continue, "Write, my child, my dear child" and so on. This song would elicit tears and sighs from many of the young women and girls in the audience. They were reminded of their old parents who were far, far away in the old country, and of how they longed to see them, but could not, except in photographs.

Then the singer would perform another folksong such as "God and his judgment are just" (*Got un zayn mishpet iz gerekht*)[191] or "Oh, little orphan, you are a tree that has been cut down" (*Oy vey yesoymele, bist an opgehaktes boymele*). The little orphans would also bring tears to the eyes of the girls and young women in the audience.

But the actress made her strongest impact when she sang a sad song about the tragedy of a girl who was "sinking into the abyss."[192] The girl tries to reach out to society to pull her out of the gutter. But society does not want to save her. On the contrary, it pushes her away, it rejects her. The girls and women wept when they heard a song such as this, and everyone, men and women alike, showered the actress with applause.

Before the evening's entertainment was over, the audience heard a moving speech from the manager. He would come out on stage to tell those assembled about the adverse conditions endured by the actors who were doing their utmost to present the finest repertoire for the entertainment and enjoyment of the esteemed audiences of Montreal. Nevertheless, people were frequenting the other movie theatres. Therefore he had to inform the audience that this situation could not go on any longer. The actors of the vaudeville theatre had to make a living, to pay room and board, and so on. Montreal Jews were therefore requested to attend the vaudeville theatre more often and bring their friends and acquaintances. Otherwise, the actors would leave Montreal and go elsewhere.

After such an appeal and warning, the audience felt obligated to revisit the theatre, not so much for the entertainment, but to keep a few poor Jewish vaudeville actors from going hungry.

Weddings

Young men and women often went to the movies. If a young man cast his eye on a girl he liked, he invited her to the cinema. Later he would ask her to the Yiddish theatre, when he had already decided that he would become her fiancé. If a young man and young woman appeared together at the Yiddish theatre everyone knew that they were engaged. Going to see a film did not have the same significance. When a young man invited a girl to a movie it did not mean that he was under any obligation to her.

After they had been to the cinema a few times, the girl would begin to sense that the young man was not indifferent to her. But she was still not certain. Only when he invited her to the Yiddish theatre did it become clear that he was in love.

Then she began to wait for a marriage proposal. If the boy was shy, she had to wait several weeks. This would cause her tremendous anxiety. When he finally proposed, she immediately informed her relatives, *landslayt*, and girlfriends, whereupon plans were begun for the wedding.

The wedding was usually arranged for a Sunday evening in a hall. The wedding party would ride to the hall in carriages. The bride and groom would ride in a carriage drawn by two horses and the parents in a carriage with one horse. Before arriving at the hall, the carriages would stop at the photographer's and the bride and groom would have their pictures taken.

The ceremony was simple. It was conducted either by an orthodox rabbi or a reverend. Under the *khupah*, the wedding canopy, no English was spoken. The bride was expected to cry as she made her way to the *khupah*, but quietly, not out loud. The groom also was supposed to look as solemn as possible.

During the wedding ceremony, the guests stood near the *khupah*. Everyone tried to stand as close as possible to the bride, the groom, and their parents. Women and girls were very anxious to see if the bride was still crying. Female guests would discuss the bride's crying. They interpreted her crying to mean that she was afraid of her future because she did not know the groom's character very well and was not certain that he would always be in love with her as now. About the groom it was said that he looked serious and worried because he was not sure that the bride would love him in years to come when he would no longer be as attractive, slim, and well-dressed as now in his youth.

During the ceremony everyone was solemn. But right after the ceremony the mood changed dramatically. The bride stopped crying and her face became radiant. The groom smiled and everyone was happy. The musicians went to work right away, and the parents kissed each other.

Immediately after the ceremony, the dancing would begin. The musicians played tunes from the old country familiar to most of the guests. The musicians, too, were immigrants who worked in sweatshops during the week, and played at weddings on Sundays.

After a few hours of dancing, the bride's parents, or the groom's parents, would clamour for the meal to begin, contending that the guests were hungry. The other set of parents did not agree. "Still too early . . . there's no fire!" they protested.

"This is scandalous! We are starving our guests!" shouted the first set of parents, becoming hot under the collar. But the other side cried, "What gluttons! This is a shame, a disgrace!"

Sometimes this type of dispute ended in a fist fight, especially when one side was from Rumania or Galicia and the others were Litvaks, Polacks, or Bessarabians.

If a fight broke out, the musicians had the task of restoring order. They would beat their drums, bang their cymbals and make such a commotion with the other instruments that the warring parents would be forced to settle down. When the musical uproar was over, the guests would march into the dining hall.

In the dining hall long tables were laden with every delicacy: smoked meat, raisins, dill pickles, peanuts, ginger ale, bananas, and homemade whiskey (water mixed with gin).

After the meal, the dancing resumed, and the wedding would end late at night. The parents and guests would send their presents after the wedding. The most prized gifts were a brass bed or a Singer sewing machine.

The day after the wedding the young couple would go on a honeymoon— not far, somewhere around the city. Their vacation would last one day. During that day the couple would travel to St. Helen's Island or Dominion Park. The park, of course, was more interesting. Going to Dominion Park was indeed a holiday for the young couple, especially on a weekday, when there were hardly any people around. The day customarily ended with a visit to the Yiddish theatre.

And that is how the young newlyweds would spend their honeymoon.

Israel Medres and Sophie Victor in 1914,
the year of their marriage.
Courtesy of Vivian Felsen.

Zionist Dreamers

ZIONISM, from a practical standpoint, was of little significance at the beginning of this century. The Zionist idea was regarded as a dream and Zionists as dreamers.

To the average Jew, the Land of Israel was a holy land, but also a desert, a wilderness. It was known as a land of holy tombs. When modern *maggidim* or Zionist agitators wanted to idealize the Land of Israel in the eyes of the masses, they would remind them of the graves of the patriarchs and the tomb of mother Rachel. They also spoke about the historical significance of the Western Wall—the holy wall. Religious Jews in their old age had the desire to go to the Land of Israel to die. When a young Jew went there to live he was looked upon as a dreamer.

Nevertheless, the Zionist dream was greatly respected as were the Zionist dreamers. Dr. Herzl, the chief dreamer, was regarded as the greatest Jew of modern times. His portrait hung in almost every Jewish home. After Dr. Herzl, Dr. Max Nordau was considered the greatest Jew and his picture was also displayed in many Jewish homes. The names of Dr. Nordau and Dr. Herzl symbolized the dawn of a new epoch in Jewish history.

In those early years, Jews donated little money to the Land of Israel, but the romantic vision of Zionism had an impact on their lives. When Jews gathered on social occasions or at concerts, they sang Zionist songs such as *Al Em Haderekh* (On the Crossroads), *Seu Tsiona* (Toward Zion), and *Bamakom Sham Arazim* (The Place of Cedars) which were then very popular. Those Jews who did not know Hebrew would sing Yiddish songs with Zionist themes such as *Es shaynt di livone, es glantsen di shtern* (The moon is shining, the stars are twinkling), or *Kum Yisrolikl aheym* (Come home, Yisrolikl).[193]

In those days, Zionist Congresses were regarded with reverence. It was common knowledge that the delegates at the congresses were prominent doctors and professors from major European cities like Paris and Berlin, Vienna and London, Budapest and Frankfurt. It was also known that these famous personalities of Western Europe had been alienated from their Jewishness but that the Zionist dream had brought them into the

Jewish camp. They had embraced the Zionist ideal because of the pressure of anti-Semitism which was manifesting itself in the universities and cultural centres of Western Europe—the same pressure which had brought Dr. Herzl[194] and Dr. Nordau to the Zionist dream. The Dreyfus case in France, the anti-Semitic mayor Dr. Karl Leuger[195] of Vienna, and the Jewish disenfranchisement in Russia and Rumania resulted in the disillusionment of assimilated aristocratic Western European Jewish intellectuals and their attraction to the Zionist dream.

The Land of Israel was still uninhabited, yet in the vanguard of the Zionist movement there were great men: Herzl and Nordau, Wolffsohn[196] and Zangwill,[197] Achad Ha'am[198] and Klausner,[199] Shmaryahu Levin[200] and Ussishkin.[201] All Jews respected these leaders for their romantic vision of the Jewish future.

Founders of the Poalei Zion (Labour Zionists) in Montreal,
July 1905, with portrait of Theodore Herzl.
Jewish Public Library.

Zionist Politics

DURING HIS LIFETIME, everyone had been interested in Dr. Herzl's political work, especially his negotiations with Turkey. Dr. Herzl had exerted every effort to obtain a charter over Palestine for the Jews. All Jews mourned his death which occurred in the midst of these negotiations.

After his death, hope appeared on the horizon. A revolutionary movement arose in Turkey in opposition to the despot Abdul Hamid and in favour of freedom, civilization, and European culture. In 1908 a coup d'état brought the civilized and freedom-loving Young Turks to power in Turkey. Zionist activists, the political heirs of Dr. Herzl, began to place their hopes on the Young Turks. Recalling that the Turks were the children of Uncle Ishmael and therefore our blood relatives, Jews felt a sense of kinship with the Young Turks.

Would the "cousins" grant us a charter over Palestine? Jewish writers in the Hebrew and Yiddish newspapers were divided in their opinions. Some believed they would grant the charter to mark the dawn of a new era of national revival and cultural rebirth for both Jews and Turks. Others foresaw a new time of troubles and imperialist wars, with intrigues against the modern Young Turks designed to draw them into a war in order to dismember the Turkish Empire. In this event, they would be unable to do anything for the Jews.

All Jews, even those not involved in Zionist activities, followed these political developments closely.

Upon arriving in Montreal, immigrants wanted to know who the Zionist leaders were. First and foremost they heard about Clarence de Sola. His personality made a forceful impression. He was respected for his lineage[202] and his high status in non-Jewish society. For a long time he was the president of the Canadian Zionists.

Clarence de Sola was also known as a successful engineer, one of the most outstanding in Canada. He was the Belgian consul in Montreal, and reputed to have inherited an extensive library from his family. As one of the most devout members of the Spanish and Portuguese Synagogue, de Sola regarded Zionism as a movement which would bring all Jews not only to a Jewish state in the Land of Israel, but back to authentic Jewish religious observance.

Among the active Zionists at that time were Chaim Bernstein, A. Levin, Louis Fitch, David Sperber, Leon Goldman, and R. Darwin.

Clarence de Sola.
"De Sola regarded Zionism as a movement which would bring all Jews not only to a Jewish state in the Land of Israel, but back to authentic Jewish religious observance."
Canadian Jewish Congress.

Zionist Radicals

THE JEWISH MASSES sang Zionist songs and revered the Zionist leaders, notably Dr. Herzl and Max Nordau. Nevertheless, they had the conviction that Zionism was a matter for certain types of European Jews, such as Hebraist intellectuals, Biblical idealists, or sentimental utopians, but not for practical people in the United States and Canada, who were busy making a living or working their way up the economic ladder.

In those days, most Jews were workers, and most of the Jewish workers were tailors or cloakmakers. An aggressive campaign against Zionism was conducted among them by socialist and anarchist trade union leaders who fought with all their might to stamp out Zionist sentiment. They claimed that Zionist theoreticians and journalists were using pro-Israel propaganda to lure the workers away from socialism and dispel their hopes for a social revolution. Zionism was disparaged and Zionist leaders were mocked in the pages of the *Forward*. It was a long time before Labour Zionism on the one hand, and the First World War and the loss of millions of Jewish lives on the other, forced the socialists to recognize the Zionist movement's right to exist in the Jewish world.

In those days anti-Zionist socialists warned the workers that Zionism was created by the bourgeoisie contrary to the interests of the proletariat which lay in class struggle and strikes. The Labour Zionists tried very hard to convince the workers not to be afraid of Zionism, that Zionism was not incompatible with socialism and would not delay or prevent the coming of the social revolution.

The Labour Zionists fought an uphill battle to be recognized as radicals and socialists. Although they, too, spoke about the social revolution, class struggle, Marxism, and the world proletariat, anti-Zionist socialists refused to recognize their radicalism. The Labour Zionists studied socialist theoreticians in order to find evidence that nationalism could be kosher and that Zionism need not be *treyf.*

The Labour Zionists found an important socialist leader and theoretician who had idealized the Land of Israel. This was Moses Hess,[204] a German Jew, one of the early great socialist theorists. But Hess had been dead for a long time and had no influence on the anti-Zionist socialists of the *Forward*. Then a contemporary Labour Zionist leader, Dr. Nachman Syrkin,[203] translated into Yiddish the classic work by Moses Hess, *Rome and Jerusalem*.[205] For a while this book was a powerful weapon which the Labour Zionists used against the Marxist anti-Zionists on the Jewish streets.

Dr. Syrkin often came to Montreal. The Labour Zionists would bring him to deliver lectures about Zionism, socialism, nationalism and internationalism. He would interpret Jewish as well as general historical events. He was an expert in Jewish historical research, a devoted Hebraist and the theoretician of Zionist radicalism.

A second important leader of Labour Zionism who often came to Montreal was Dr. Chaim Zhitlovsky.[206] Zhitlovsky, just like Syrkin, was a thinker and theoretician, but while Syrkin had come to radicalism through Zionism, Zhitlovsky was first a radical and then a Zionist. Syrkin had begun to speak to Jews in Hebrew, while Zhitlovsky started with Russian. Syrkin became a Zionist radical while Zhitlovsky became a radical Zionist. Both Syrkin and Zhitlovsky preached and explained Zionist ideals to the Jewish masses and succeeded in breaking down the anti-Zionist fortresses which the early socialists and anarchists had erected.

In his early lectures Zhitlovsky took the position that nationalism must be completely separate from religion. However, many disagreed with him and religious Jews were afraid of him. Shortly thereafter he modified his stand on religion and maintained that the Torah contained social truths which had historical value, even for free thinkers.

Later he began to lecture about the prophets and linked them to the socialism of Karl Marx and the class struggle. His lectures were attended not only by workers and radicals, but also by Hebrew teachers, foremen from the clothing shops, and self-employed businessmen. Zhitlovsky "discovered" that Isaiah was a socialist, just like Karl Marx or Lassalle,[207] and that Amos was a courageous fighter against the capitalists, namely, the princes and rulers of his day.

Under the influence of Zhitlovsky and Syrkin, the Labour Zionists and other radical nationalists began to study and research Jewish history. They began to seek, and find, socialist and radical tendencies among the prophets, the commentators of the Mishna, and even among the founders of Hasidism. They "discovered" that the Hasmoneans and other factions and groups who rebelled against the Romans were brave revolutionaries just like the revolutionaries who fought against the czar in Russia. Many people attended Zhitlovsky's lectures not to learn about partisan socialism, but for a modern interpretation of Jewish history.

In the first decades of this century Dr. Zhitlovsky was at the forefront of modern nationalism. He inspired Labour Zionist groups in various cities, including Montreal, to found schools for national radical education. He played a leading role in the organization of the congress movement in the United States and Canada which came into existence after the First World War and which was one of the most important achievements of the early radical Zionists.

Moses Hess (1812-1855)
The first Zionist socialist, his book *Rome and Jerusalem*,
became a classic of Zionist literature.

The Historic Zionist Convention

IN THE DAYS when the class struggle was a dominant theme in the Jewish immigrant community, Zionist activity was also sharply divided. The Labour Zionists agitated for a socialist Zionism while the general Zionists carried on their own separate work which consisted of collecting money (small amounts at a time) for the Jewish National Fund and selling shares in the Zionist Colonial Bank, which had its head office in London.

Since the Labour Zionists devoted themselves mostly to propaganda and agitation, their work was more evident to the new immigrants who heard about the general Zionists mainly when a Zionist convention was taking place.

Let us take a moment to see what a Zionist convention would have looked like in the old days. We shall use as an example the eighth convention, held in Montreal in September, 1908, which came to be designated historic because it was held soon after the revolutionary coup d'état in Turkey. The seizure of power by the Young Turks raised great hopes among the Zionist leaders of the time.

On the day prior to the opening of the convention, an editorial appeared in the *Keneder Adler* greeting the delegates on the occasion of their meeting at a "historic moment." The editorial expressed great joy at the downfall of Turkish despotism and the hope that the collapse of Abdul Hamid's regime would bring salvation to the Jews. One could not negotiate with Turkish despots whose promises were virtually worthless, continued the editorial. Now, however, a new age was dawning. Communication would be possible with the progressive and civilized leaders of the Young Turks, and Herzl's dream would be realized.

In the same issue of the newspaper, prominence was given to a report from New York. There the Turkish consul had attended a meeting of the Labour Zionists and delivered a very stirring speech which caused a sensation in American Zionist circles. Among other things, he said, "Our people and the Jewish people will go hand in hand. Our religion and the Jewish faith are alike. Jews are able businessmen, financiers, literati, and artists — you will revitalize the Land of Israel. You will bring light and progress to every corner. We, the Turks, will defend you for the sake of our common interests."

The next day the *Keneder Adler* came out with large headlines which read "Inspired Zionist Convention." The smaller captions read: "All the cities and towns of Canada are represented at the convention ...The convention understands the importance for Zionism of the current situation in Turkey...Ten-year-old delegate arouses a burst of enthusiasm."

The highlight of the first session was the message from Clarence de Sola,[208] the president. In his message, de Sola spoke of the historic juncture which Zionism had reached thanks to the revolutionary changes in Turkey. The delegates were very moved, sensing the great responsibility which the historic moment had placed upon them. De Sola concluded that the time had truly come to begin to build the Jewish homeland and called upon the delegates present to meet their national responsibility by making every effort to find financial support for the building of Eretz Israel.

On the second day the convention closed with a banquet in Victoria Hall in Westmount. The mood was exalted, the atmosphere festive. Everyone felt inspired and elevated by the historic moment and the glowing prospects for the realization of the Zionist dream. The speakers were Clarence de Sola, Reverend Dr. H. Abramowitz,[209] Lyon Cohen,[210] Rabbi N. Gordon,[211] Mr. Leo,[212] and Rabbi Zvi Cohen.[213] The report in the *Keneder Adler* emphasized the fact that Rabbi Cohen spoke in Yiddish.

Almost all the speakers stressed that now was the time when large amounts of money had to be collected for the building of the Land of Israel. The original plan was to raise the sum of fifty dollars at the banquet in order that the name of the President, Clarence de Sola, would be inscribed in the "Golden Book." In the end, considerably more was raised. The enthusiasm was so great that those present gave much more than could have been anticipated. According to the report in the *Keneder Adler*, the amount of $125 was collected. This was a huge sum to have been raised at a Zionist banquet in those days. There was such elation, reported the newspaper, that the banquet lasted until three o'clock in the morning.

Incidentally, this convention had two other salient features, which should be noted. First, a letter from David Wolffsohn, president of the World Zionist Organization, was read which generated much excitement among the delegates. In this letter Wolffsohn expressed the hope that the recent change in government in Turkey would be propitious for the Jews and called the outlook for Zionism optimistic.

Secondly, Lazarus Phillips, a ten-year-old delegate, a student at the Talmud Torah, inspired the delegates with his speech. The young delegate spoke in the name of his Zionist youth group, *Zeirei Zion*, and appealed for the construction of a new building for the Talmud Torah to provide the children with better ventilation and improved sanitary facilities. The *Keneder Adler* reported that for several minutes after the young Phillips had concluded his speech, the delegates were overcome by enthusiasm.

The day after the convention the *Keneder Adler* printed an editorial which posed the following question. Why did the masses, namely, the immigrant Jews, not come to Fraser's Hall to attend the convention? The editorial writer had a piece of advice for the Zionist leaders, namely, that they should begin to think about ways and means of involving the Jewish masses in the problems of the Land of Israel and in the Zionist movement in general.

Rabbi Zvi Hirsch Cohen

Politics and Citizenship

DURING THE PERIOD of mass immigration, newcomers were constantly aware of their new-found freedom and equality in Canada. In comparison to Russia or Rumania, they found Canada a veritable paradise insofar as its treatment of Jews was concerned.

However, in certain neighbourhoods, especially Griffintown[214] and Pointe St. Charles, there were street gangs who would bully Jewish immigrants, insult them, and beat them. These hoodlums were young men who frequented the burlesque theatre where so-called "Jew comedians" would mock the newly arrived Jews, thereby arousing disdain and hatred toward Jewish immigrants.

As a result, members of the Jewish community began to take an interest in city politics. They reckoned that this vile bullying would stop if a Jewish alderman were sitting on the city council where he could demand more police protection against the anti-Semitic ruffians. However, in order to elect a Jew to the city council, it was necessary to have a large number of Jewish voters. Thus the Citizens' League was founded to persuade the immigrant Jews to become naturalized Canadian citizens.

The organizers of the Citizens' League were well-known in the Jewish neighbourhood. They socialized with municipal politicians, knew the mayor and some of the aldermen, were friendly with Jewish lawyers, and made speeches at the mass meetings which the League very often convened in the Labour Temple. The meetings would take place on Sunday afternoons. For the immigrant Jews these mass meetings were of great interest. Among the leaders of the Citizens' League who were well-known to the immigrants for their political connections and activities were Joseph Miller, Benny Steyerman, and Chaim Steinman.

A mass meeting of the Citizens' League was conducted more or less in the following fashion. Five or six people would be seated on the podium. One was a Christian who was either an alderman or a member of the Legislature. For Jewish immigrants he was a symbol of a friendly Canadian citizen. The chairman would introduce him as one of the *khside-umes-ho-*

oylem, the gentile friends of the Jews, adding that if ever a Jew in Montreal needed a favour, he should come to this Christian. He would conclude his introduction by asking the audience to stand.

The Christian would deliver a short speech wherein he expressed satisfaction that Jews from Russia or Rumania had come to Canada. Assuring those present that their personal freedom and cultural autonomy would be respected, he advised them to become naturalized citizens of this free country as soon as possible.

Among the other speakers was a lawyer. The audience also stood as he was introduced. A lawyer in those days was among the elite as there were very few Jewish lawyers. In the eyes of the Jewish immigrants he was an aristocrat. It was easy for them to recognize that he was a person engaged in noble, non-physical work.

The immigrants would listen to the lawyer with great respect and rapt attention even though his Yiddish was not particularly fluent. He spoke about Canada and the tremendous opportunities here for everyone. He would describe how easy it was for all Jews to send their children to high school and then to university. When he spoke about university he would give himself as an example. His parents had been Jewish immigrants. His father had begun as a worker. His mother lit candles every Friday night. However, his father, being a practical man, quickly became a citizen by taking out citizenship papers. He advised the immigrants, whom he addressed as "my very dear friends," to be as practical as his father.

The other speakers would also make a strong impression on the audience. One, who had the appearance of an immigrant, contrasted the bullying gendarmes and *uryadniki*[215] of Russia and Rumania with the friendly policemen in Montreal. The Montreal police, he would emphasize, do not stop Jews in the street and demand their passports. One does not need a passport in free Canada. Nevertheless, citizenship papers, he would conclude, are necessary. With citizenship papers one could go anywhere—to Parliament, the Legislature, or City Hall.

At a mass meeting such as this there would appear a speaker with an oratorical style employing the type of language which contemporary writers used in their books and pamphlets: *ci-vi-li-za-tion, e-man-ci-pa-tion, con-sti-tu-tion, assi-mi-la-tion, na-tion-al-ism, Zion-ism* and so on. This speaker would refer to great personalities such as Spinoza, Disraeli, Sir Moses Montifiore, Dr. Herzl, Baron Gunzburg,[216] Captain Dreyfus, Jacob Schiff,[217] and Max

Nordau. He denounced assimilation and obsequious politicians, and demanded that Russia adopt a *con-sti-tu-tion* ensuring freedom and equality; he attacked the enemies of Captain Dreyfus in France, and noted that these were the same people who were enemies of *e-man-ci-pa-tion, re-nais-sance,* and *hu-ma-ni-ty.* He reminded the audience that without Disraeli, the British would not have had an Empire. He congratulated the Jewish immigrants from Russia for coming to a country where there were no Purishkeviches or Krushevans.[218] In Canada, he concluded, Jews must become naturalized in order to win *re-pre-sen-ta-tion* in City Hall, in the Legislature, and in Parliament.

This speaker had a profound impact on the newcomers. After a mass meeting such as this, Jews who were already on their way to becoming Canadianized, would fill out application forms for citizenship.

The first concrete result of the citizenship campaign became evident in 1912, when a Jewish businessman, Abraham Blumenthal,[219] was selected as a candidate for alderman. There were already enough Jewish voters to elect the first Jewish alderman in Montreal. This paved the way for the election a few years later of the Jew Peter Bercovitch[220] to the Quebec Legislature followed by the election of the Jew S. W. Jacobs[221] to the Parliament of Canada.

Academic Anti-Semitism

WHEN THE FIRST Jewish alderman was elected in 1912, Montreal Jews were jubilant. They counted on their representative at City Hall to demand that the police adopt strict measures to put a halt to anti-Semitic street incidents. This was indeed what happened.

However, another type of anti-Semitism persisted. This was not the anti-Semitism of the street bullies, but an intellectual or academic anti-Semitism. This was the anti-Semitism of a small group of conservative, ultra-nationalist French Canadian intellectuals.

The immigrant Jews in Montreal knew little about this type of anti-Semitism for they had not experienced it. Similarly, the vast majority of the French Canadian population was unaware of this sort of anti-Semitism. Newly arrived Jews found the French Canadians in the cities and towns of the Province of Quebec to be most hospitable. In the days when Jewish immigrants ventured out to the countryside as peddlers, most villages were inhabited exclusively by French Canadians. They received the Jews in a friendly manner, communicating with them in sign language. The French Canadians did all they possibly could to ease the hard work of the peddlers. Thanks to the hospitality and cooperation they encountered, many peddlers, after a short period of travelling through rural areas, were able to settle down in small towns, open stores, and live among friendly neighbours.

However, as I mentioned, there was a small group of conservative nationalist anti-Semites in the Province of Quebec who were inspired by foreign, not local, influences, and particularly by extreme reactionaries in France. These Quebec anti-Semites occupied themselves with writing anti-Jewish articles in weekly newspapers which were published under various names in Montreal and Quebec City. Already in existence in the 1870's, these publications had carried anti-Semitic articles even before there was a significant Jewish population in Canada. One of the anti-Semitic weeklies, *La Croix*, was published in Montreal and circulated throughout the province.

The writers for *La Croix* and other similar weekly publications claimed that they were defending the prestige and authority of the Catholic Church.

They maintained that the position of the Church was being undermined by the cultural upheaval in the wake of the industrial revolution in Europe. As conservatives they were terrified of Western European democratic politics and the liberal ideals being propagated by modern political movements.

In Canada these conservative elements fought fiercely against the liberal influence of Sir Wilfrid Laurier, who had revitalized the Liberal Party in the Province of Quebec. Fearing that immigration from Europe would introduce pernicious political and cultural notions, they became bitter opponents of immigration. Because of the massive Jewish influx, they became even more antagonistic toward Jews.

Extreme reactionaries from France, in those days called papists, exerted the strongest influence on the anti-Semites in Canada. In claiming to defend the Catholic Church, the papists behaved as though they were holier than the pope and hence their name. The intellectual leader of the papists in France was Edouard Drumont, the editor of *La Libre Parole*. The anti-Semitic articles in Edouard Drumont's *La Libre Parole* were reprinted in anti-Jewish journals and newspapers in other countries. For a time he was the ideologue and theorist of anti-Semitism. A bitter enemy of the Talmud and all the religious works of the Jews, Drumont perceived the essence of Judaism as a danger to conservatism and reaction. He saw in world Jewry a powerful force for liberalism, scientific progress, and cultural advancement.

A small group of papists and extreme anti-liberals in Montreal read *La Libre Parole* and reprinted Drumont's articles in their weekly papers. These weeklies did not have a large readership and had little effect on most sectors of the population. In the period of mass immigration, when Sir Wilfrid Laurier was Prime Minister of Canada, the papists were a small minority in the Province of Quebec.

The vast majority of French Quebecers enthusiastically embraced the authentic liberalism to which Laurier had introduced them. Jewish immigrants were also deeply affected by the liberal ideas of Sir Wilfrid Laurier. In the *Keneder Adler* much was written about his sympathy for the Jews and other oppressed peoples. The *Keneder Adler* also occasionally reported the anti-Semitic articles written by the papists in *La Croix* and other similar weeklies.

The *Keneder Adler* carried stories about Henri Bourassa, the leader of the Quebec nationalists, who from time to time would make public pronouncements against the Jews. Bourassa's anti-Semitism was milder than that of Drumont, but its impact was greater than that of the writers of *La Croix* or the other weeklies. For a long time, Bourassa was the editor-in-chief of *Le Devoir* and a member of the Parliament of Canada where he opposed a resolution protesting against the Russian government for inciting pogroms against the Jews.

Only those few Jews who knew how to read French were aware of the anti-Semitism of the elite. Among them were a handful of Jewish lawyers, who were concerned with Jewish social conditions, such as S.W. Jacobs,[222] Peter Bercovitch,[223] Louis Fitch,[224] and Marcus Sperber,[225] as well as writers for the *Keneder Adler*, who took upon themselves the task of responding to the anti-Semitic articles in the French weeklies.

S.W. Jacobs was elected to Parliament, representing
Montreal's Cartier riding, in 1917.

The Attack on the Talmud

ALTHOUGH DURING THE PEAK period of immigration the impact of academic anti-Semitism in the country as a whole was minimal, Jews who were able to read the anti-Semitic weekly publications in Quebec City and Montreal became worried. They feared that with time their influence could become stronger and even dangerous.

It was, of course, difficult to combat this intellectual anti-Semitism. No laws prohibiting academic anti-Semitism existed in the Province of Quebec nor in the rest of Canada. Only in 1910 did a case arise as a result of which academic anti-Semitism would be challenged in a court of law three years later. It should be noted that the anti-Semitism in this instance was more than academic. It bordered on incitement to a pogrom.

The events occurred in Quebec City where one of its residents, the notary Plamondon, in March of 1910 delivered a lecture on the subject of Jews. Speaking before a Catholic audience, he viciously attacked the Talmud. He claimed that the Talmud commanded Jews to fight Christians, and that Jews all over the world, including Quebec, lived according to the dictates of the Talmud and consequently hated Christians.

Plamondon's lecture was printed in the Quebec anti-Semitic weekly *La Libre Parole*. Subsequently the publisher of this weekly issued it as a separate pamphlet which was circulated in and around Quebec City.

The residents of Quebec City considered Plamondon to be a fanatical papist and loyal follower of Edouard Drumont, the anti-Semitic ideologue from France. In fact, Plamondon's speech about the Talmud was lifted directly from Drumont's articles published in anti-Semitic journals and books. At the time Drumont was regarded by anti-Semites around the world as the authority on the Talmud and Judaism. He was the leader of the reactionaries and anti-republicans in France.

The most virulent claims against the Talmud in Plamondon's pamphlet were as follows:

The Talmud commanded Jews to regard Christians as idol-worshippers.

The Talmud permitted Jews to violate Christian women.

The Talmud gave Jews a free hand to cheat Christians in business and to charge them usurious interest rates.

The Talmud permitted Jews to murder Christians. If, after killing a Christian, a Jew felt remorse, the Talmud said that in order to ease his conscience, the Jew should consider that he had killed an animal, not a human being.

As this pamphlet began to circulate among its Christian residents, the Jews of Quebec City had the impression that their Christian neighbours were avoiding them and that Christian customers were patronizing their businesses less frequently. In the streets Christian youths insulted Jews and even attacked them. If a policeman arrested a young man for assaulting a Jew, the assailant was given a citation in the Catholic weekly *L'Action sociale catholique* which was edited by the priest, Abbé D'Amours.[226] Young hoodlums attacked the synagogue while people were at prayer, throwing stones and breaking windows.

Quebec Jews became alarmed and Jewish community leaders in Montreal were deeply disturbed. They felt that they could no longer remain silent. They convened at the Baron de Hirsch Institute to decide on a course of action. They resolved to sue the two anti-Semites, Leduc and Plamondon, for slander.

The task of conducting the case against the two anti-Semites was entrusted to S. W. Jacobs, who was then one of the most distinguished lawyers in Montreal. In addition to being an outstanding jurist, Mr. Jacobs was also very active in the Jewish community, a leading figure in the Baron de Hirsch Institute, and a prominent member of the Liberal party. Prime Minister Laurier knew him well and wanted him to sit in Parliament as a representative of the Jewish community. A few years later he was elected as the first Jewish member of the Parliament of Canada.

Mr. Jacobs, the senior lawyer for the Jewish side, was assisted by Louis Fitch. Mr. Fitch was one of the first Jews to graduate from McGill University with a gold medal and a scholarship. To Jewish immigrants he was known not only as a lawyer, but also as an influential member of the Zionist movement. For many years, he was vice-president of the Canadian Zionist Organization and a captivating speaker at Zionist conferences.

The Jewish side was also represented by a famous Quebec solicitor,

L. Cannon, a partner in the law firm of Alexander Taschereau,[227] who for a number of years was the Premier of Quebec. The plaintiffs were two Quebec City Jewish businessmen, Benjamin Ortenberg and Louis Lazarovitch. They were claiming $500 in damages for the harm they had suffered as a result of the impact of the anti-Semitic pamphlet which Plamondon had written and Leduc had printed.

When the case came to trial, Quebec was divided. Some people sided with the Jews, others with the anti-Semites. Among liberals there was sympathy for the Jewish side. In reactionary circles a sympathetic attitude to the anti-Semites was evident. At the outset of the trial Reuben Brainin wrote in the *Keneder Adler*:

> The court action against the anti-Semites signifies that the Jews of the Diaspora have begun to stand tall. The suit demonstrates that Jews no longer bow before their enemies. They do not ask for mercy from those who slander them nor do they seek to vindicate themselves before those who libel them. Instead they fight back. They conduct themselves as dignified, proud people with self-respect. They expose the anti-Semites to the public, tear off their pious masks and reveal them in their true light so that all the world can see that they are small, unworthy souls who use lies and fabrications to achieve their inhuman and antisocial aims.

The trial against the anti-Semites, Leduc and Plamondon, began on the 19th of May, 1913 in the Quebec Superior Court. Interest in this case, both in the province and in the rest of the country, was unusually high. Even non-Jews recognized the historic nature of this trial. People realized that this was not merely a dispute between two plaintiffs, Ortenberg and Lazarovitch, on the one hand, and two defendants, Leduc and Plamondon, on the other, but that the court had to decide between the Jewish community and the anti-Semites.

Both Jews and non-Jews were aware that this litigation was between the Talmud and those who were conducting a campaign of libel and defamation against it, between liberalism and dark fanaticism. People realized that this trial would determine whether or not it was permissible to openly incite against the young Jewish community in Canada and to spread lies and calumnies about Jewish immigrants designed to hinder their integration into the country which had so warmly welcomed them.

For the non-Jews of the Province of Quebec the trial symbolized the dramatic conflict between reactionary, ultraconservative elements, and the Liberals who already enjoyed strong support in the province under the leadership of Sir Wilfrid Laurier who had introduced liberalism to French Quebecers.

There were two issues before the court: First, whether it was true that the Talmud taught Jews to hate, cheat, and even murder Christians, and secondly, whether an individual Jew could claim damages when the entire Jewish people was the object of a libelous attack but no individual Jew was named.

The anti-Semites called three expert witnesses to prove that everything they had written and printed about the Talmud was true. The witnesses were the priests Abbé D'Amours, Abbé Nadeau,[228] and Abbé Grandbois.[229] They also expressed their opinions on Jews in general and one of them linked the Jewish faith to ritual murder.

The Jewish side had experts on the Talmud as well. The chief expert witness was Rabbi Dr. H. Abramowitz. A second important expert witness for the Jewish side was Reverend F.G. Scott,[230] rector of the Anglican St. Matthew's Church in Quebec City.

All the expert witnesses for the defence relied on the French anti-Semitic theorist Edouard Drumont, as did Plamondon. When he took the stand, Plamondon conceded under oath that he himself knew no Hebrew and that everything he knew about the Talmud he had learned from Drumont and Lamarque,[231] two Frenchmen notorious for their theories on Judaism. He stated that he believed everything Drumont had written about the Talmud and about the Jews. In court Plamondon explained that he had delivered his lecture not on his own initiative, but was requested to do so by the priests of St. Roch Church and the members of the Catholic Charest Club where the lecture was held.

Abbé Grandbois spoke as an historian and a specialist on the Talmud, Jewish history, and Judaism. The Talmud, he claimed, contained a tractate on idolatrous worship entitled *Avodah Zarah*, which is filled with hatred toward Christians. In this connection, he told the following story:

In the year 1590 in Warsaw there took place a meeting of rabbis. On the agenda was the question of what to do about the tractate on idolatry, the *Avodah Zarah*. Because of this tractate, the rabbis feared that Christians would turn against the Jews. They therefore decided to take the entire *Avodah Zarah* out of the Talmud and commit it to memory, so that the Christians would have no evidence against the Jews.

Abbé Grandbois' story was discredited immediately. On the table in the courtroom was a copy of the complete Talmud. The lawyers for the plaintiffs easily proved that the *Avodah Zarah* was still part of the Talmud and therefore the expert's story was not authentic.

The lawyers for the plaintiffs, S. W. Jacobs, Louis Fitch, and L. Cannon, had no difficulty whatsoever in rebutting the expert evidence of the three priests whom the anti-Semites had called as witnesses. Abbé Nadeau maintained that everything that was written in Plamondon's pamphlet was the truth. He declared that he had studied the Talmud and the work of Drumont and Lamarque. When the lawyers for the Jewish litigants cross-examined him, he admitted that there were authorities on the Talmud who opposed Drumont and Lamarque. When he was asked if he had read those authorities, he replied that he had not. Asked why not, he stated that being a teacher in a Catholic college, he earned only $100 a year, and could not afford to buy more books on the Talmud or the Jews.

The third expert witness was Abbé D'Amours, editor of the weekly *L'Action sociale*. Abbé D'Amours raised the matter of ritual murder. The Jews, he said, use Christian blood for religious purposes. When asked if he knew that certain cardinals had disproved the libel that Jews use Christian blood for ritual purposes, the priest claimed not to know. This same expert spoke of Jewish conduct in Canada. The Jews, he contended, were guilty of obstinately clinging to the Jewish faith and not wishing to assimilate into the majority of the population. To this the lawyer Jacobs replied with the following ironic comment: "How should the Jews convert, to Catholicism or to Protestantism? According to the opinion of Abbé D'Amours, the Jews of the Province of Quebec should convert to Catholicism, whereas in other provinces where the majority are Protestants, the Jews would have to become Protestants."

The evidence of the anti-Semitic experts on the Talmud was demolished by the experts called by the plaintiffs, Rabbi Dr. Abramowitz and Reverend Scott. On the day that the priests gave their evidence against the Talmud,

Reuben Brainin wrote in his editorial in the *Keneder Adler:* "What is going on here? In what century are we living? Today in the 20th century, in the free country of Canada, judges and lawyers are dealing with the question of whether we Jews are cannibals and whether the Talmud is an encyclopedia of robbery and murder."

In the same year that the Plamondon case was heard in Quebec, the historic blood libel trial against Mendel Beilis[232] took place in Kiev. A great deal of the evidence about the Talmud which the czar's prosecutors used against Beilis was used by the lawyers for Leduc and Plamondon at the Quebec trial. Mr. Jacobs, the senior lawyer for the Jewish side, did indeed draw a parallel between the trial in Kiev and the case in Quebec in his closing arguments. He described how the civilized world was outraged by the czarist regime's revival of the blood libel against Jews, unearthing once again the medieval accusations against the Talmud. He demonstrated that the defence of the anti-Semites in Quebec was based on the same malevolent calumnies and falsehoods as the prosecution of Mendel Beilis in Kiev.

Mr. Jacobs said that the Quebec trial had touched every Jew in Canada. All Jews, he contended, were being accused by the anti-Semites of belonging to a criminal sect which permitted the cheating and murder of Christians. Jews in the whole country were waiting for the accusation to be declared false and libelous by the court.

Mr. Jacobs spoke sarcastically of Edouard Drumont whom the experts for the defence had characterized as a learned authority and social philosopher. "Drumont was a journalistic acrobat," Mr. Jacobson said. He described him as an "adventuristic careerist" who took advantage of the anti-Jewish mood of obtuse and ignorant people at the time of the Dreyfus trial to make a career for himself preaching hatred toward the Jewish people.

The chief expert for the Jewish side was Rabbi Dr. H. Abramowitz. His task was difficult and delicate. Before going to Quebec City, Rabbi Abramowitz consulted with Rabbi Zvi Cohen and other important Talmudists on the preparation of his expert evidence for this case. In the courtroom Rabbi Abramowitz gave a general overview of the essence of the Talmud. He quoted many passages to show how the Talmud teaches Jews to treat Christians with special friendliness. He pointed to the great moralistic value of the Talmud and the pervasive role it played in Jewish life in difficult times when the Jewish people were surrounded by enemies who wanted to annihilate them.

A strong impression was also made by the Christian clergyman Reverend Scott, who testified for the plaintiffs. Reverend Scott also spoke disdainfully about the anti-Semitic experts. Their testimony regarding the Talmud, he said, belonged to archeology. Hundreds of years ago the libel against the Talmud and Jews had already been disproven. The lies and slander had been stored away in the archeological cellars of history whence the anti-Semitic experts had retrieved them and placed them before the court in Quebec City.

For weeks the newspapers in the Province of Quebec were full of long, objective articles on the trial. Public opinion was divided. Amongst non-Jews there was a debate as to which experts to believe, Abbé Nadeau or Reverend Scott, Abbé D'Amours or Rabbi Abramowitz.

In the *Keneder Adler*, Reuben Brainin wrote in an editorial that the expert evidence of Rabbi Abramowitz was of great value. He regretted that the Jewish masses knew little about the Talmud and reproached Jewish lecturers for holding forth on Darwin, Ibsen, Spencer, Karl Marx, Tolstoy, and Maeterlinck, while neglecting the Talmud. Only Zhitlovsky, on one occasion, had given a lecture about the Talmud, lamented Brainin.

The lawyers for the defence, of course, were not silent, and there were a good many of them. There was no shortage of lawyers who believed it their duty to defend the anti-Semitic principles and slogans of Drumont, Leduc, and Plamondon. One of them, Mr. Bédard, argued that the Jews were a world problem. An eternal hatred toward the Jewish people prevailed and that hatred was natural. In all countries one could find groups of people who detested the Jews. To this argument Mr. Jacobs responded that only dark and fanatical elements harboured any hatred toward the Jews. These dark elements aroused the instincts of backward people and incited them against helpless Jews for anti-Semitic purposes.

The lawyers for the defence relied, for the most part, on a legal technicality, namely, that an individual had no right of action where a group to which he belonged was slandered. This argument was a strong one. The lawyers Cannon and Fitch contended that although no individual was named, nevertheless the anti-Semitic agitation of Plamondon and Leduc was directed against every Jew in Quebec City, especially as the Jewish population consisted of only eighty people in a city of 80,000. To support his position,

Mr. Fitch cited the following example from the jurisprudence.

In France extreme heretics had conducted an anti-clerical campaign. In one instance a writer who was an aetheist, wrote an article about a certain Catholic convent in which he accused the 800 nuns of debauchery. One nun sued the writer for libel. In his defence the writer claimed that he had not named the plaintiff and therefore she could not sue him. The nun won her suit. The court ruled that although the writer had attacked a group, the nun was a member of that group, and therefore she had been harmed.

The Superior Court judge accepted the argument of the lawyers for the defence. He therefore ruled that the plaintiffs, Ortenberg and Lazarovitch, did not have a right of action where the entire Jewish community was targeted, and he rejected the Jewish claims. But the case did not end there. The Jewish side appealed his decision. The historic case came before the Court of Appeal which rendered the final judgment.

Rabbi H. Abramowitz
Photo by Notman.
From *The Jew in Canada* by A. D. Hart, 1926.
Canadian Jewish Congress Archives.

The Historic Decision

THE TRIAL of Leduc and Plamondon took place in May of 1913. The final judgment was handed down nineteen months later, at the end of December, 1914. The decision, which constituted a historic victory for the Jewish side, was rendered not in the court of the first instance, but by six judges in the Court of Appeal.

In the Superior Court where the trial took place, the Jewish plaintiffs were unsuccessful. The judge ruled that an individual had no right of action where a group to which he belonged was harmed. The plaintiffs appealed to the Court of Appeal, and there the outcome was entirely different.

The six judges of the Court of Appeal, after examining the evidence which both parties had presented to the Superior Court, rejected out of hand the arguments of the anti-Semites. In their lengthy judgment, they emphasized that Leduc and Plamondon had failed to substantiate their accusations against the Jews and the Talmud, and that they had no right to spread libel against the Jewish people in such a way as to incite hatred against Jewish citizens. Sitting on the Court of Appeal were Chief Justice Sir Horace Archambault, the Honourable Mr. Justice N. V. Trenholme, the Honourable Mr. Justice Joseph Laverne, the Honourable Mr. Justice A. G. Cross, the Honourable Mr. Justice H. G. Carroll, and the Honourable Mr. Justice L. P. Pelletier.

The Court of Appeal judgment quoted from Plamondon's brochure to demonstrate that certain opinions expressed therein were dangerous, namely the false claims made against the Talmud. The judges found that the aim of the defendants was not simply to express abstract philosophical ideas about the Talmud, not merely to conduct an academic debate over the collective beliefs of the Jewish people. Instead, their intent was to harm Quebec Jews by inciting hatred and hostility. The law could in no way vindicate them. Jewish citizens were entitled to the full protection which the state could and should afford them. The judges emphasized the fact that Canadian Jews had enjoyed equal rights since 1838 when Hart[233] was elected to the Legislature, and that it was the duty of the courts to protect their rights.

This decision was a triumph for the Jews of Canada. It was a victory not only over the two defendants, Plamondon and Leduc, but over a sizeable group of intellectual anti-Semites in the Province of Quebec who had wished to transplant to Quebec soil the international anti-Semitism of Drumont and Lamarque, then prevalent in reactionary circles in many European countries, and to impose it on the Catholic Church.

For the Jewish side the two anti-Semites, Leduc and Plamondon, were not important. The plaintiffs forgave the judgment which the Court of Appeal had awarded against the defendants in damages. After the final decision, the defendants claimed to be impecunious and isolated individuals without the means to satisfy the judgment.

During the nineteen months between the beginning of the trial and the final judgment, an event of great consequence occurred which affected every country in the world and had a profound impact on the Jews of Europe. The First World War erupted throwing most of the peoples of Europe into a hellish inferno. By the time the judgment of the Court of Appeal was delivered in the Plamondon case, the war was raging.

In the year before the outbreak of World War I, the Beilis trial took place in Kiev. This trial, which occurred a few months after the Quebec trial, captured the attention of the entire world, including Canada. The Beilis case symbolized the dramatic conflict between reaction and liberalism in Europe. Although czarist Russia was then the bastion of reaction on the European continent, liberal influences were already having an effect on the Russian people. Russian literature had become a significant part of European culture. In the Beilis case, Russian reaction was dealt a severe blow. That case was also a defeat for the anti-Semites of other countries.

In 1913, during the time of the Plamondon trial in Quebec, the Jews of Montreal received an important guest, Nahum Sokolov.[234] His visit was a major event in the Jewish community here. It was the first time that so important a guest had visited Montreal. He was welcomed with tremendous respect. He was taken to City Hall where he was given an official reception. For the first time the city officially welcomed a Zionist leader from Europe.

Sokolov addressed a general mass meeting in His Majesty's Theatre.[235] He also spoke at a meeting of Hebraists. At the mass meeting he dealt in extensive detail with the situation of the Jews in Europe in 1913, on the eve of World War I. The following is the picture which Sokolov painted of the state of the Jews at the time.

Anti-Semitism reigned in almost every country of Europe. While in some countries the anti-Semitic groups were small, in others they controlled entire political parties. On the one hand Europe was witnessing the advance of liberalism together with technological, cultural, and scientific progress. But on the other hand, the forces of reaction, racism, and anti-Semitism were gaining ground.

In Western Europe anti-Semitism had thrust the Jewish question to the forefront. Certain Jewish groups had sought to resolve the Jewish question through assimilation, but anti-Semitism prevented this. The Jewish question, argued Sokolov, must and could be resolved only through the establishment of a national home in the Land of Israel. In those days great Zionist leaders like Sokolov were forced to do battle not against the British Colonial Office, nor against the Arab League, but against Jewish anti-Zionists who sought the path to assimilation rather than to the Land of Israel.

As for Canada, Sokolov said, "In Europe until now we considered Canada a wilderness as far as Jewish life was concerned. Now that I am here, however, and I see the people who are the leaders of Jewish society, I say that Canada already has a healthy Jewish community of which much can be expected."

Nahum Sokolov, Reubin Brainin, and I. Yampolsky at the offices
of the *Keneder Adler* on Main Street near Ontario.
From the *Keneder Adler*'s Golden Jubilee Edition, 1957.

The Children's Strike against Anti-Semitism

DURING THE TWO YEARS immediately preceding the First World War the Montreal Jewish community grew significantly. By 1912 there were already many Jews who were fluent in English, interested in local problems, and knowledgeable about current events elsewhere in Canada.

In the schools of the Jewish neighbourhoods, Dufferin and Aberdeen, there were so many Jewish children that they began to outnumber the non-Jews. For some disgruntled Protestants, this state of affairs was intolerable.

From time to time their discontent would find expression. Indeed, on one occasion, an anti-Semitic remark by a teacher triggered a strike by Jewish children. This occurred in Aberdeen School, where in March of 1913 there were about 500 Jewish children enrolled. A teacher had made a remark about Jews which had offended the Jewish children in her class. During the recess, the children of all the classes heard about it and spontaneously decided not to remain silent. On the spot, the 500 children quickly resolved to proclaim a strike.

In closed ranks, boys and girls of all ages, marched out of the classrooms and across the road to St. Louis Park. There the strikers held a mass meeting where they appointed strike leaders as well as a committee authorized to speak and negotiate on behalf of all the children. Two resolutions were adopted. The first required that the children from all classes maintain solidarity and not return to school until authorized to do so by the strike committee. Anyone breaking rank would be considered a scab. In those days, when the majority of the children were from working-class families, even the small children in the first grade felt contempt for scabs. Secondly, the children demanded that the anti-Semitic teacher be dismissed from her job.

Rabbi H. Abramowitz and H. Wolofsky came to settle the strike. After conferring with the strike committee in St. Louis Park, the strike head-quarters, they negotiated with the school administration. Although the school authorities sympathized with the grievance of the striking children, they did not wish to accede to their demand to dismiss the teacher. This would create a precedent for school children to achieve their ends through strikes. Instead, they promised to transfer the teacher to another school after some time had elapsed.

The mediators came back to the strikers and relayed the school administration's offer. At first the strikers were not satisfied. Rabbi Abramowitz and H. Wolofsky tried to convince them that the offer was fair under the circumstances and that it amounted to a victory for the Jewish children. The strikers were finally convinced that they had won the strike, especially after being assured that there would be no reprisals against the leaders of the strike. Shoulder to shoulder the children, led by Rabbi Abramowitz and H. Wolofsky, marched back into their classrooms.

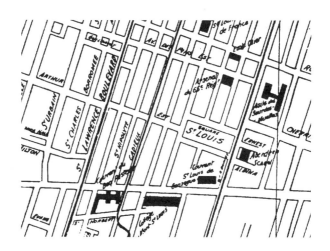

In March, 1913, protesting an anti-Semitic remark made by a teacher, five hundred students of all ages marched out of Aberdeen School on strike and held a mass meeting in St. Louis Square.

Yiddishism and Hebraism

IN THE PERIOD when the Jewish population was steadily increasing, the number of Jewish children enrolled in the public schools grew as well. Although some Jewish children also attended the Talmud Torah, the percentage of children who received a Jewish education was still very small. However, in the few years prior to the First World War, significant advances were made in the field of Jewish education. As the cultural level of the Jews gradually rose, more people began to take an active interest in Jewish education.

Among the *maskilim*, Zionist activists, and Hebraists who upon arriving in this country became active in the Talmud Torah were Yitzhak Gold and Benjamin Weiner. They strove to improve the quality of Jewish religious education. In the pre-war years many religious Jews already had greater expectations with regard to Jewish education. They were no longer satisfied with their children learning to recite the *kaddish* and chant the *Haftarah*. There was a demand for classes in Bible and Jewish history. Hebrew literature also appeared on the curriculum.

By 1912 the Labour Zionists had become active in the field of Jewish education. The first National Radical School was founded in 1911. This school, however, failed to satisfy all the members of the Poalei Zion. The language struggle had split the Labour Zionists into two factions. One group, espousing Zhitlovsky's views that Yiddish was the language of the Jewish people, believed that children must be educated in Yiddish. The second faction saw Yiddish as the mother tongue and the language of the Jews in the Diaspora, whereas in the Land of Israel only Hebrew would be spoken. Their position was based on Syrkin's ideas.

The language conflict was then very real. Both Syrkin and Zhitlovsky often lectured publicly on this subject. Zhitlovsky was the originator of Yiddishism and Syrkin the theorist of Hebraism. Zhitlovsky relied on the idealism and revolutionary struggle of the Jewish masses who spoke Yiddish, whereas Syrkin drew his inspiration from the idealistic spirit and social teachings of the prophets who had spoken Hebrew.

Although at first the language debate was academic in nature, when plans were drawn to build the National Radical Children's School, it became a serious practical problem. The Labour Zionists came to the realization that they could not be united in one school. Two schools were needed.

As a result, in 1914, the Hebraist Labour Zionists founded the Jewish People's School (Yidishe folk-shule). In the National Radical School (now the Peretz School) the first teachers were W. Chaitman[236] and H. Noveck. Among the first teachers in the Jewish People's School were Dr. Yehuda Kaufman,[237] Shloime Wiseman,[238] A. S. Sachar, M. Mikhlin, Shlomo Gold, and M. Dickstein.

While non-religious middle-class and working-class Jews sent their girls to the radical Jewish schools, their boys attended the Talmud Torah. Although some radical parents did send their sons to the radical schools, for a long time it appeared that the Talmud Torah had been founded especially for boys and the radical schools especially for girls.

Teachers of the National Radical School, 1915.
Dr. Chaim Zhitlovsky is in the first row, third from left.
In the back row are W. Chaitman (first from left) and
H. Noveck (third from left).

Cloakmakers

IN 1912 AND 1913, tailors and cloakmakers represented a large part of the Jewish population. In Montreal cloakmaking, or the manufacture of women's clothing, began to develop as a trade about fifty years ago, and the men's clothing trade, tailoring, somewhat earlier.

In the pre-World War I period, women dressed differently than they do today. Suits were more fashionable than dresses. To sew a suit for a woman was complicated and delicate work. Therefore cloakmakers were held in high regard among the immigrant Jews. An older Jew would be very proud to have a son-in-law who was a cloakmaker.

Cloakmakers were the aristocrats among the workers. They earned higher wages, they were better dressed, attended the Yiddish theatre more frequently, purchased Jewish books more often, and in summer sent their wives to St. Sophie or New Glasgow.

Younger cloakmakers took great pride in their union. The Yiddish newspapers often wrote about the Cloakmakers Union. A cloakmakers' strike in New York or Philadelphia was a major news event for Jews throughout the United States and Canada. In New York the Cloakmakers' Union was under the leadership of prominent Jewish socialists and community leaders such as B. Schlesinger, Morris Hillquit, Professor Isaac Halevy Hourwich, Meyer London and L.D. Brandeis.[239]

The International Ladies Garment Workers Union played a prominent role not only in the economic sphere, but in the social and cultural life of the immigrant Jewish workers as well. Among the younger cloakmakers were many intelligent and knowledgeable socialists who attended lectures, posed questions and carried on debates with the lecturers.

The cloakmakers were always well-organized and well-paid, but they were not wealthy people. Only a handful were able to save enough money to purchase their own homes or to send their children to high school or university. Although the cloakmakers earned a decent living, their employment was seasonal. Between seasons they were unemployed and were forced to use their savings and even incur debts.

In its early years, the Cloakmakers Union in Montreal was affiliated with the Industrial Workers of the World which was an extremely radical organization. Well-known among the first officials of the Montreal Cloakmakers Union were its chairman, N. Rambach, and its secretary, S. Liebenson. After the 1912 general strike, which the union lost, it was weakened considerably. At that point the cloakmakers demanded that the union re-affiliate with the International Ladies Garment Workers Union. The switch was made, and under the ILGWU the Cloakmakers Union was reinvigorated. For a long time Joseph Schubert served as general secretary of the revitalized union. Years later factional differences developed between the left and the right which completely paralyzed the functioning of the union. Finally, in 1934 the ILGWU sent Bernard Shane here to reorganize the union, and with the help of several Montreal cloakmakers, the union was again rejuvenated.

Beckie Berger and Rachel Birnbaum worked in the
needle trade in Montreal.
Archives of Ontario A04778, F1405-23-103,
MSR8427 #3

Tailors

By 1912 tailors in Montreal were well-organized. Their union was revitalized through the initiative of several people, especially H. M. Caiserman.

When Caiserman immigrated to Canada, like many other immigrants from Rumania, he was advised to work in a men's clothing shop. In Rumania he had been active in the syndicalist movement, attracting the suspicion of the reactionary Rumanian government. Concerned about his personal safety, he left the country and came to Canada where he went to work in a tailor shop.

In the shop Caiserman witnessed the helplessness of the non-unionized workers. Having experienced the detrimental atmosphere of the sweatshop, he soon left to organize the tailors with the aim of improving their economic situation and raising their social status. At Elstein's bookstore, a centre for radical idealists, he conferred with Elstein on a course of action to organize the tailors. A few weeks later, Caiserman had become the leader of a revived Tailors Union.

After a few years the Tailors Union had 4,000 members and led a general strike which was one of the most violent strikes in the history of the men's clothing industry in Montreal. In 1912 the tailors officially worked 59 hours a week. Unofficially, during the busy season, they worked from dawn until dusk. The tailors called a strike to abolish the 59-hour work week as well as other unacceptable working conditions. The strike lasted for nine weeks. The *Keneder Adler* reported at the time that every third person in Montreal was affected by the strike.

To support the strikers, a huge demonstration was organized in the city in the form of a parade with several marching bands. The *Keneder Adler* described the parade as follows. At one o'clock in the afternoon the parade set out from the Champs de Mars. Leading the parade was a marching band followed by Chief Marshall Barsky and Assistant Marshall Aronstein. Behind them marched the members of the strike committee followed by all the women employed in the trade. This was the first division of the march. The second division consisted of all the cutters and workers from

the Gardner, Kellert, and Vineberg shops led by a second musical band.
The third division consisted of the workers from the Freidman Company and the Levinson, Standard, and Semi-Ready shops. In the fourth division were the workers of Friedman Brothers, Wener and Hart, Union Clothing and Elkin's shop. All the workers from the smaller shops marched in the fifth division.

The parade snaked its way from the Champs de Mars along St. Denis Street up to Sherbrooke, from Prince Arthur, along Main, back to Sherbrooke, up to Windsor, back to Dorchester and to Main again, and from there to Coronation Hall.

In those days the tailors were militant and aggressive. The bosses, however, were also ready for a fight and even recruited strike-breakers from other cities.

To be sure, a strike of such magnitude injected considerable acrimony into Jewish community relations and exacerbated the existing class divisions between workers and employers. It also resulted in a number of factory owners setting up shop in the smaller towns of Quebec to avoid unionized labour.

The 1912 strike ended in victory for the workers. The 59-hour work week was abolished. The tailors' existence became somewhat easier. From then on they never worked more than 49 hours a week and began to dream of a 44-hour work week. That dream would eventually be realized in 1919.

In 1916 the Tailors Union joined the Amalgamated Clothing Workers of America. Previously it had been affiliated with the United Garment Workers of America, which was under the American Federation of Labour.

The largest and most bitter strike led by the Amalgamated in Montreal was the general strike of 1917.

On the Eve of the Storm

By 1914 Montreal already boasted an important Jewish community with an array of Jewish schools, charitable organizations, cultural institutions, Jewish bookstores, and social and political groups representing every contemporary ideology.

A Jewish clinic, the Herzl Dispensary, opened in 1912. A year later, the Mount Sinai Sanitorium was founded. The idea of a Jewish General Hospital was conceived at this time and realized years later when the General and Maternity Jewish Hospital was constructed on Côte St. Catherine Road. The *Keneder Adler* had initiated the drive for the hospital. Alan Bronfman was the first and current president of this institution.

In 1913 Jewish immigration from Russia and Rumania was still substantial, but immigrants were no longer the majority of the Jewish population. Most Jews were already acculturated. A fair number of Jewish students attended university, and many Jews were interested in Canadian politics.

The number of Jewish students had grown to the extent that at Queen's University in Kingston the administration had wanted to take measures to exclude Jews. Loud Jewish protests, not only in Montreal, but throughout Canada, forced the university's directors to abandon their plans for the anti-Semitic *numerus clausus*. That was in 1912.

In the same year, for the first time, a Jew, A. Blumenthal, was elected alderman in Montreal. But when a second Jew, Marcus Sperber, Q.C., tried to win a seat in the provincial legislature, he failed.

Although in 1912 there were not enough Jewish voters to elect a Jew to the Quebec Legislative Assembly, in the provincial elections four years later Peter Bercovitch was successful. A year later, in 1917, S. W. Jacobs became a member of the Parliament of Canada in Ottawa.

Radical Jews also got involved in politics, campaigning vigorously against bourgeois Jewish politicians. In those days the radicals took little notice of the ongoing problems facing the city, the province or the country. They considered such issues unworthy of the full attention of intelligent and socially conscious people at a time when they were expecting the coming of the revolution and, in its wake, an ideal world where current problems would resolve themselves. The radicals used election campaigns to agitate for their ideals and aims and to explain to the workers what economic and social life would be like on the morrow of the social revolution.

A bitter feud continued to rage among the radicals as to whether the revolution would also solve the Jewish question in the Diaspora. The general socialists believed it would, but the Labour Zionists disagreed. The latter maintained that the social revolution would solve all the problems of the workers, but not those of the Jewish people.

Thanks to this theoretical debate, during one municipal election campaign two radical candidates actually ran against each other, Joseph Schubert for the general socialists and H. M. Caiserman for the Labour Zionists. Harold Laski, then on the faculty of McGill University, was the spokesman for Caiserman. A famous socialist from New York, Jacob Panken, campaigned on behalf of Schubert.

In 1912 the radicals achieved an alliance long enough to publish the *Folkszeitung*, a weekly newpaper devoted to the interests of the workers. The radical intellectuals of that time congregated around the *Folkszeitung*. Leon Chazanovitch (Katriel) was the editor. But the *Folkszeitung* would not exist for long. The adherents of the various radical factions managed to remain united for only a few months.

The non-partisan intelligentsia gathered around Reuben Brainin who personified the Hebraism of Vilna and Odessa in combination with the Western European culture of Vienna and Paris. Although he loved the progressive, militant youth, he disapproved of the noisy class struggle being fomented by the radicals. He sought dignity and refinement even in the conduct of strikes.

In 1912, during the general strike called by the tailors, the *Keneder Adler* published an open letter to the editor complaining to Brainin that he paid too little attention to the strike in his editorials. The letter was signed by M. Shneur, a prominent Labour Zionist activist.

Brainin replied in a lengthy editorial that although he was on the side of the strikers and supported their demands in his editorials, "I am a staunch opponent of a system which teaches the workers invective, abuse, envy, hatred, and vengeance." And he added, "Where the seeds of hatred and jealousy are sewn, neither noble ideals nor lofty sentiments can grow. An atmosphere poisoned by hatred, contempt, invective, and oaths can only cripple the human spirit and make people blind and deaf to their own interests.

"The Jewish masses are as dear to me as my own flesh and blood," Brainin continued in the editorial, "but I bear no animosity toward Jews who belong to other classes. I consider them all as brothers, Jews, and human beings. Among Jewish capitalists there are intelligent, moral, good-hearted, noble and fine people."

Brainin came to Montreal not only to be a writer and an editor. He was also a community leader and educator. To the social milieu in which he traveled he brought refinement and sophistication. He was an aristocrat in both appearance and comportment. Devotees of belles-lettres, Hebraists and Zionist visionaries gathered around him.

The cultural environment which Brainin had inspired exerted its influence on broad segments of the Jewish community long after Brainin had left the *Keneder Adler* and returned to New York. Young poets and journalists arrived on the scene. The poet J.I. Segal was discovered at this time. The first book of Yiddish poetry to be printed in Montreal was Segal's. His name quickly became known in literary circles in New York and in Yiddish literary circles all over the world where his talents as a poet were highly esteemed.

J.I. Segal (1896-1954)
Courtesy of Syliva Lustgarten.

The First World War

THE OUTBREAK of World War I was sudden and unexpected. At the time no one could have imagined such a catastrophe. Although people informed about European politics knew that the international situation was bleak, they did not anticipate that it had deteriorated to such an extent that it could trigger a world war which would drown Europe in blood.

After the wars between Turkey and the Balkans, it was known that the balance of power in Europe had shifted and that the great powers were divided into two enemy camps competing against one another for political influence, colonial possessions, and world markets.

The two enemy alliances, Germany and the Austro-Hungarian Empire on the one hand, and Russsia, England, and France on the other, could resolve their differences only through a world war. The signal came from Sarajevo where the Austrian Crown Prince was assassinated.

For the Jews of Europe, the First World War brought the most devastating losses in modern Jewish history. No one then could have foreseen that some years later the rise of Nazism and World War II would bring destruction a thousand times more tragic.

The Jews in the Russian Empire, which at that time included much of Poland, suffered the most in the war. Although they had languished under czarist rule, they had enjoyed a cultural life of such vitality that its influence was felt by Jews the world over.

Prior to 1914, Warsaw, Vilna, and Odessa were centres of Yiddish and Hebrew culture. In Lithuania were to be found the famous yeshivas of Telz, Volozhin and Slobodka, which provided rabbis to Jewish communities not only in Russia, but all over the world.

In the cities and towns of Russia Hebrew high schools had been established. Hebrew and Yiddish literature flourished, and the Jewish press had expanded in new directions. This cultural efflorescence was cut down in its entirety in the bloody years of World War I.

In the few years before 1914 the Zionist movement had fashioned closer ties among Jewish communities all over the globe. The Zionist Conference was the unofficial parliament of nationally conscious Jews in every part of the world. The Great War shattered this national unity. Zionists from Warsaw, Odessa, and London had to sever relations with Zionists in Berlin, Vienna, and Prague.

The war literally split the Jewish people. Jewish soldiers in the Russian army had to fire upon Jewish soldiers in the German army. Jews in British uniforms became the enemies of Jews who served Franz Josef, the Emperor of Austria and Hungary.

The war in Europe had strong repercussions in Montreal. Canada entered the war to help the motherland. At the very outset, the Jews of Canada realized that tremendous devastation would befall the Jewish communities of Europe and that the war would destroy a large and significant part of the Jewish people.

Before long tragic reports were received about the Jews of Russia. The worst fears regarding their fate at the hands of the anti-Semitic czarist regime materialized. Russian generals declared all Jews to be enemies of the state. Jews were treated mercilessly by the Russian troops as they fled into the interior of the Russian Empire pursued by the victorious Germans. Only in Galicia was the Russian army victorious. On the other fronts the Russian armies were routed, and in beating a retreat they took out their frustration on the Jews.

The Jews in Montreal, as in other large cities in North America, felt that they had to come to the assistance of the Jewish victims of the war by organizing themselves in such a way as to be able to bring the greatest measure of relief to the suffering European Jews.

In the first year they did not yet know what to do or how to organize for the relief effort. All ties between the Jews in North America and the Jews in Eastern Europe had been severed. Canadian Jews felt a dual loyalty, first to their country, and secondly, to the afflicted Jews of Europe who were the tragic victims of the war. They felt tremendous rage and hatred toward the czarist regime, but their patriotic duty to their country demanded that they keep this hatred to themselves for the time being.

In Canada the declared aim of the war was "to make the world safe for democracy." Jews embraced this slogan and hoped that when the war was won, the entire world would become democratic and the czarist regime would either disappear or reform itself. The majority of Jews expected that it would be reformed. No one could have foreseen that there would be a revolution in Russia which would destroy czarsim and wipe it off the face of the earth. They had thought that a revolution could only happen in a country which was losing a war but not where the enemy was losing.

Thanks to the war, life in Canada changed tremendously. New industries for the war effort were created. The fact that people began to work more and earn more had an impact on Jewish life. The tailoring shops, which were almost entirely in Jewish hands, began to manufacture uniforms. New people found employment in the sweatshops. Others left the shops to work in the munitions factories where various weapons were being produced, especially bullets for heavy artillery to defeat the Kaiser and make the world safe for democracy.

Jewish soldier Abraham Charney, Montreal.
Archives of Ontario F1405-23-103

The War Years

IN THE FIRST YEAR of the Great War, Jewish community activity intensified. The war impelled even those who were previously indifferent to take an interest in community affairs and feel directly involved in the dramatic events affecting the entire world. Each day the papers came out with sensational headlines about the harrowing events on the war fronts. To such news no one could remain indifferent.

The *Keneder Adler* began to appear twice a day and every copy was snatched up at once. Yiddish-speaking Jews could not get their fill of news from the front lines. German troops were penetrating further into Russia, and Russian troops were in Galicia. Jewish cities and towns in Poland, Lithuania, Byelorussia, the Ukraine, and Galicia figured prominently in the newspaper reports about the war, and Jews who had relatives in those cities and towns became increasingly dejected. Immigration had come to a complete standstill.

In Montreal the impact of the war was keenly felt. Large ammunition plants were hastily erected in Montreal's suburbs. Older and middle-aged people went to work in these factories, while young people enlisted in the army. All signs of unemployment virtually disappeared.

At that time there was a demand for workers in the ammunition factories where shells were made for heavy artillery. People were well paid. Small businesses grew large and big businesses larger still. Small companies merged into large corporations.

Notable changes also occurred in "Jewish" trades and businesses. During the war years the Jewish middle class grew significantly, while some middle class Jews entered the wealthy upper class.

A number of tailor shops began producing military uniforms which meant easier work. But the life of the skilled worker became more difficult. Similarly in the cloakmaking trade the situation deteriorated. As women in the war years began to dress more simply, the need for qualified workers began to decline. Discontent among the tailors and cloakmakers led to frequent strikes. In 1917, while the pace of work accelerated in all trades, both the tailors and the cloakmakers called general strikes which erupted in violence in the Jewish streets. Especially disruptive was the tailors' strike.. The tailors' strike lasted for two months. Almost every day there was fighting on the picket lines. Public opinion was hostile to the strikers. The police and the English-language press, as well as the French press, took the position that it was not patriotic to strike during a war. Joseph Schlossberg, the general secretary of the Amalgamated, came from New York to lead the strike but his main task became to deny the accusations in the English-language newspapers that the strike was being led by foreigners.

Jewish community leaders were extremely uncomfortable with the strike which they believed reflected poorly on the Jewish population as a whole. S. W. Jacobs and other prominent community leaders, as well as the *Keneder Adler,* made every effort to convince the factory owners to come to an agreement with the union. The mayor of the city and the members of the Board of Control also got involved, and a committee of Jewish businessmen was established to help the strikers.

The strike was finally settled with the tailors winning the principle of the closed shop and a forty-nine-hour work week instead of fifty. Two years later, in 1919, the tailors succeeded in obtaining a forty-four-hour work week much more easily the one hour reduction in 1917. Although the cloakmakers' strike was settled much sooner through arbitration, both sides lost. Following that strike the cloak trade suffered a decline due to the above-mentioned fact that women were buying fewer suits.

While the problems of the war took precedence in the life of the community, local matters were not neglected. During this period a strong revival on the cultural front was evident. As a consequence of the war young people were less interested in petty party politics and became more involved in non-partisan Jewish issues and cultural concerns.

When in 1915 the great humourist Sholem Aleichem came to Montreal, his visit was a major event and a grand celebration of culture in the city. More people attended the reading he gave at the Princess Theatre than the hall could hold. An even larger crowd honoured him at a banquet.

To a certain extent the class divisions between uptown and downtown divided the Jewish intelligentsia. When I.L. Peretz died, two memorial gatherings were held in Montreal, one in Prince Arthur Hall, and a second at the Baron de Hirsch Institute.

The most important cultural institution at this time was the Jewish Public Library which was founded in 1914. The outstanding personalities involved in the library were Reuben Brainin and Dr. Yehuda Kaufman.[240] They both had a great influence on Jewish cultural life, especially because their approach to culture was non-partisan. Dr. Kaufman embodied the popular appeal of Hasidism, the romance of Hebraism, and the ethics of socialism. Later on he left Montreal for the Land of Israel where to this day he devotes himself to the study of culture. Also active in the library during the Brainin-Kaufman period were L. Zuker, Joseph Eidelberg, Eliyahu Greenberg, S. Belkin, and H. M. Caiserman. They were later joined by S. Katzman, S. Temkin, Nahum Meyerson, I. Halperin, and Israel Rabinovitch.

Sholem Aleichem's visit to Montreal in 1915 with the committee of the Jewish Public Library.
Seated to the left of Sholem Aleichem (white hat) are Reuben Brainin and Dr. Yehuda Kaufman.

Jewish Soldiers

As SOON as volunteers began to be recruited for the Canadian army in the fall of 1914, Jewish boys in Canadian uniforms appeared on the streets of Montreal. Although these young people were extremely unhappy that czarist Russia was an ally of England and Canada, nevertheless they enlisted in the army. They hoped that the British government would convince the czar to cease persecuting the Russian Jews and grant them equality.

Some community leaders even formulated a plan to establish a separate Jewish regiment. After much debate, it came to naught. Reuben Brainin wrote a lengthy editorial in the *Keneder Adler* decrying this plan, warning that it was dangerous "to celebrate one's own private Sabbath" and advised Jewish boys to enlist in the already existing Canadian regiments. This is indeed what Jewish young men did.

A year after the war broke out, in September of 1915, there was already a sizeable group of Jewish volunteers at Val Cartier, the military base near Quebec City. A Jewish delegation comprised of Rabbi Zvi Cohen, S.W. Jacobs, and H. Wolofsky, travelled from Montreal to visit the Jewish soldiers. They met with the Jewish volunteers, participated in a prayer service with them, and arranged for them to take leave on the High Holidays. While the Montreal delegation was in Val Cartier, a group of Jewish soldiers was already on its way to England with the 60th Battalion.

The demand to found a separate Jewish military unit persisted. In 1916 the Minister of Defence, the Honourable Sam Hughes, authorized a Jewish officer, Captain Isidore Freedman, to recruit a special Jewish regiment as part of the 206th battalion. The other officers in this regiment were Lieutenants Herbert Wineberg, Alex Solomon, Charles Lesser, Sol Rubin, and Albert Freedman. In June of 1916 the first recruitment meeting for the Jewish regiment was held at the Baron de Hirsch Institute during which Lyon Cohen, Peter Bercovitch, Captain Isidore Freedman, Lieutenant Marcus Sperber, and others spoke.

Four hundred young men enlisted in the Jewish regiment which was sent to England at the end of 1917. There they were divided into various

units. Most served in France while others were sent to Gallipoli, Meso-
potamia, Solonika, and Egypt.

In the newspapers, one often read about Canadian Jewish war heroes.
Among the Montreal Jews who had distinguished themselves was Captain
William Sebag-Montefiore. The newspapers reported that he had single-
handedly captured seven German officers. Sebag-Montifiore served in a
British cavalry unit which took part in the conquest of Palestine.

World War I recruitment poster.
Jewish Federation of Toronto, Ontario Region Archives.

Jewish Legionnaires

After the Balfour Declaration in November of 1917, a movement began in Montreal to create a Jewish Legion which would fight under the British against the Turks to liberate the Land of Israel for the Jewish people. The organization of the Jewish Legion was a major development in Jewish Zionist politics in the aftermath of the Balfour Declaration. Montreal was the centre of this great event and to Montreal came Jewish youth from cities all over Canada to serve in the Jewish Legion.

The first call to young people printed in the *Keneder Adler* read as follows:

The great moment has arrived! After a thousand years of persecution and oppression we are now recognized as a nation, as a people equal to other peoples. This momentous occasion has entrusted us with great responsibilities. With our blood we must seal our alliance with England and the other nations which granted us recognition. The Jewish Legion is the first manifestation of our redemption. Young and old, rise up to do battle for your people! To arms! For the freedom of your people and country!

The Jewish Legion for Palestine was part of the British, not the Canadian, army. In March of 1918, the Canadian military authorities granted permission for Canadian boys to enlist in the Jewish Legion. Two months later the first group was sent to a military base in Windsor, Nova Scotia where the legionnaires received their training.

The first group of legionnaires was organized following a meeting of the Labour Zionists where the guest speaker was Yitzhak Ben-Zvi[241] who is currently the Chairman of the National Council in Eretz Israel. Ben-Zvi was then known among the Labour Zionists but not in other circles. Even the Labour Zionists could not have imagined that he would one day play a leading role in Israel. He came to Montreal to serve in the Legion. Upon his departure a farewell evening was arranged in his honour at the home of A. Parnes, who was then one of the active members of the Labour Zionist

Organization.

David Ben Gurion also came to Montreal to serve in the Jewish Legion. As a prominent Labour Zionist leader, he also was feted with a farewell evening where men and women made speeches in his honour. Yet none of the speakers could have foreseen that this legionnaire would one day become the head of the Zionist agency and a candidate for the first Jewish president or prime minister of a Jewish homeland.

Other prominent Jews served in the Legion. A special recruiting commission for the Legion arrived here which consisted of Joseph and Moses Brainin, Gershon Agronsky, and Louis Fisher. They held recruitment meetings in order to attract more young people into the Legion. Bernard Joseph, who is now a well-known figure in the Jewish Agency, played an important role in the Legion. For a time he was in charge of the recruiting office in Montreal. He himself was a legionnaire.

Over fifty young men from Montreal served in the Jewish Legion, undergoing the entire training process from the camp in Windsor, Nova Scotia to the military bases in Eretz Israel.

David Ben Gurion in British uniform as a member of the Jewish Legion. In May, 1918, Ben Gurion arrived in Canada for military training with other volunteers.

Relief Committees

IN 1915 MONTREAL JEWS began to organize relief for the victims of the war in Europe. The news of the war was devastating. In Russia the German armies were advancing and Russian generals were expelling Jews from the areas close to the front lines. When the Russian troops lost a battle, they took it out on the Jews. When they won a battle, as in Galicia, they also went after the Jews.

In Montreal, as in all other cities in the United States and Canada, Jews were extremely distraught. As many as 600,000 Jews were fighting against the Kaiser's army to help make the world safe for democracy. At the same time, pogroms were being perpetrated against Jews in Russia. Jews cursed the czar, but were forced to do so quietly. The czar, after all, was an ally. His troops also were fighting for democracy and against "Kaiserism." The Jews had to bite their tongues and be silent. They hoped that perhaps the czar would change. In the non-Jewish press friendly articles were being written about the czar who was described as a decent, good-hearted person, who loved all his subjects. And his subjects had so much affection for him that they called him Batyushka (Father). The non-Jewish newspapers also warmly endorsed Nikolai Nikolayevich, the commander-in-chief of the czar's army, describing him as an excellent strategist. His troops, nevertheless, were in retreat, and the further they retreated, the more the Jewish communities suffered.

In Montreal it was not yet known exactly how to assist the victims of the war, but the community began to organize for this purpose. Religious Jews founded the Central Relief Committee, radicals created the People's Relief Committee, and wealthy uptown Jews set up the Canadian Jewish Committee.

In the fall of 1915 the first direct appeal came from Lord Rothschild[242] and Lord Swaythling[243] on behalf of the Jewish war victims. In a very short time $60,000 was raised. In the spring of 1915 a people's conference was held in Prince Arthur Hall which was attended by representatives of 65 organizations. There the *Folksfarband*, the Canadian Jewish Alliance, was founded with Reuben Brainin as chairman and Dr. Yehuda Kaufman as secretary.

To collect money, the Canadian Jewish Alliance distributed black boxes to Jewish households. Every Sunday it sent boys and girls as part of a volunteer relief army door to door to collect the coins from the black boxes. The Canadian Jewish Alliance also did political work, such as sending a petition requesting England to pressure czarist Russia to cease the persecution of Russian Jews.

The Alliance undertook to organize all the Jews of Canada into a Council of Communities. At the same time the Zionist Federation also decided to convene a Jewish Conference for the purpose of unifying Canadian Jews as well as formulating Jewish demands to be presented at the peace conference. Bitter rivalry ensued. The Jewish Conference was held in November, 1915.[244] A delegation of the Canadian Jewish Alliance attended the conference, putting an end to the dispute. The Alliance reached an agreement with the Central Relief Committee and the Canadian Relief Committee to work harmoniously for the purpose of relief.

In December of 1916, the Central Relief Committee held a large mass meeting in the Monument National Theatre to raise money on behalf of the Jewish war victims. The guest speaker was Rev. Zvi Hirsh Masliansky[245] from New York, renowned in the Jewish world as a popular Yiddish preacher, whose speeches could indeed move hearts of stone.

The theatre was packed. A few other important speakers also participated, among them Rabbi Zvi Cohen, Rabbi Dr. H. Abramovitch and Louis Fitch. But it was Rev. Masliansky who touched people's hearts and caused Montreal Jews to weep openly. When he began to describe the plight of the Jews in Russia loud wailing was heard in the theatre as young and old wept. The next day, the *Keneder Adler* reported:

All the emotions that had been bottled up in the hearts of Montreal Jews for the past two and a half years, since the beginning of the war, poured out yesterday afternoon at the mass meeting for relief in the Monument National Theatre. When Rev. Masliansky began to speak about the Jewish war victims, the entire crowd broke out in sobs. A cry of lament filled the hall. Men and women put their heads down on the arms of their chairs and cried unrestrainedly.

Rev. Masliansky was not speaking about the millions of Jews who died in gas chambers. He was not talking about entire Jewish communities which were annihilated. The Jewish tragedy of which he spoke cannot be compared to that which would take place in the Second World War. Rev. Masliansky described how Jewish families in Vilna and other cities were mourning their loved ones who had perished in the war. He spoke about synagogues in towns and cities like Yekaterinoslav[246] which were converted into military barracks or stables for horses. When the audience heard these tragic facts they could not control their emotions and when the appeal for funds was made, women emptied their purses and threw all the money they had into the hats of the collectors. When someone mentioned that other valuable items, such as jewelry, were being collected, women took off their earrings and tossed them into the hats, along with their rings and watches.

At the end of 1916 while the Jews of Montreal were crying in the Monument National Theatre over the suffering of the Jews of Russia, they could not have imagined that a worse fate would befall the Jews than that suffered under the rule of the czars. Unfortunately they were tragically mistaken. One year later, in 1917 and 1918, following the Bolshevik Revolution, the civil war in Russia unleashed horrendous pogroms and massacres, particularly in Poland and the Ukraine, which made the pogroms and persecutions up to and including the year 1916 seem like child's play.

Zionist War Policy

WITH THE OUTBREAK of World War I, the international Zionist network was shattered. Zionism, as a political movement, was in crisis. The situation was particularly acute for Jews in the Allied countries because Palestine was under the control of the Turks who sided with Germany in the war.

In 1915 Zionist leaders in Montreal came to the realization that Zionism would have to change its political orientation. Instead of relying on Turkey, it would be better to depend on England. The Zionist Federation decided to convene a conference not only of Zionists, but of all Jews, to formulate this new orientation. The conference would bring together Jews from all over Canada for two purposes: first, to demonstrate their loyalty to Canada and England, and secondly, to express the wish that England liberate Palestine from the Turks and provide the possibility for the Jewish people to build a national homeland there.

The conference was held on the 15th of November, 1915 in the Gayety Theatre. It was the first large gathering of Canadian Jews, both Zionists and non-Zionists.

Because the conference was an historic occasion for the entire Zionist movement, it was attended by the most prominent American Zionists such as Louis D. Brandeis, Jacob de Haas, and Abraham Goldberg. But the most important guest of all was Dr. Shmaryahu Levin, a leading figure in world Zionism. Delivering his speech in Hebrew, Dr. Levin gave his enthusiastic endorsement to the new Zionist political orientation, which had been formulated in Canada.

Another distinguished guest at the conference was the Honourable Arthur Meighen, a member of the federal cabinet. He thanked the Jews for their loyalty to England and declared that after an Allied victory, the Jewish people would certainly be treated with fairness and justice. The most important resolution passed at the conference was addressed to England, requesting assistance in establishing a Jewish homeland in Eretz Israel once the war was won. For the first time, at this conference, American Zionist leaders gave their whole-hearted approval to the alliance of political Zionism with England.

In 1916 this new Zionist policy was adopted in the United States. The mood of American Jews in the first years of the war had been entirely different from that of their Canadian counterparts. American Jews bitterly opposed the anti-Semitic regime of the czar. As the United States was a neutral country, American Jews were not obligated, as were the Jews of Canada, to support England while they were hostile to England's Russian partner. A Zionist policy in support of England could not have been adopted at the time in the United States and therefore it originated in Canada.

By the end of 1916, however, the situation had changed. German victories were coming to an end. German militarism revealed its frightening brutality. When the Germans sank the *Lusitania*, they provoked hostility in many who had previously been neutral or friendly to Germany. Sympathy for England was strengthened. American Zionists also began to place their hopes on England.

In the spring of 1917 the British Foreign Minister, Lord Balfour, visited Canada before spending several days in Washington with President Wilson. Upon his arrival in Ottawa, he invited Clarence de Sola to meet with him. However, as De Sola was ill at the time, their meeting did not take place in Ottawa but in Washington several days later. De Sola returned from Washington elated. Balfour had told him that England was about to make a public announcement to the Jewish people concerning Eretz Israel. De Sola said that Balfour had shown him a preview of the planned declaration.

The official Balfour Declaration was proclaimed in November, 1917. Zionist leaders in Montreal discussed among themselves the fact that the official declaration was much weaker than the version which de Sola had been given by Balfour in Washington. They believed that after Balfour had met with de Sola, he had conferred with President Wilson about Eretz Israel. President Wilson had already consulted with three prominent Jews, Rabbi Dr. Cyrus Adler, Julius Rosenwald, and Bernard Baruch, all non-Zionists. Unofficially it was rumoured that as a result of President Wilson's consultation with the three non-Zionists, the official Balfour Declaration was considerably diluted.

After the Balfour Declaration strong opposition to Clarence de Sola germinated among Montreal Zionists. De Sola maintained that the Balfour

Declaration had resolved the problems of political Zionism, and that henceforth the rest could be left to England. Those opposing him believed that this was only the beginning of political activity. Younger Zionists were very disappointed with de Sola's position and accused him of wanting to liquidate political Zionism. Among the opposition were Louis Fitch, Michael Garber, Benjamin Weiner, and Bernard Joseph.

In 1919 a Zionist Conference took place in Toronto. There the opposition won its battle against De Sola. De Sola resigned and A. J. Freiman took his place. A. J. Freiman's wife, Lily Freiman, founder and president of Hadassah, also became part of the leadership. With the Freimans a new chapter began in the story of Canadian Zionism.

The Freimans were unassuming egalitarians. At the same time, however, they had connections in the government, and among the political and philanthropic elite of Ottawa. Mrs. Freiman played a leading role in relief work. The Freiman house in Ottawa was a meeting place where the luminaries of the Zionist movement would often congregate to plan various important Zionist ventures.

In the beginning, A. J. Freiman attracted a great deal of attention with the large contributions he made to Eretz Israel. Later, when people got to know him more intimately, they valued him not only as a great philanthropist, but also as a leader who poured his heart, his soul, and all his energy into every endeavour. Under his leadership Canadian Jews made significant strides on behalf of Eretz Israel.

At the same time, Mrs. Freiman introduced the Hadassah movement to Jewish communities all over Canada. Under Mrs. Freeman's leadership, Hadassah raised large amounts of money for various initiatives in Eretz Israel.

The Freimans came to be known, loved, and respected in the world Zionist movement and in Eretz Israel. They were instrumental in establishing closer connections between the Jews of Canada and the pioneers in Eretz Israel who were building the Jewish homeland.

Real Estate

BETWEEN 1914 AND 1918 substantial changes occurred in the economic life of the Jews of Montreal as the city grew significantly. Because of the war new factories were built which attracted people from the surrounding towns and villages. New houses were constructed, new roads dedicated, and new neighbourhoods flourished.

As the city began to expand, a real estate boom drove up the prices of empty lots and houses. Many Jews began to deal in real estate. They purchased houses, sold them quickly, bought others and sold them. At the time it was easy to purchase a house and resell it at a profit. Jews with small amounts of capital, from one to two thousand dollars, could easily become involved in real estate. Those without capital became real estate agents working on commission. There were agents who had sub-agents all over the city. Anyone could become a sub-agent, even those who knew nothing about selling houses. All they had to do was to identify a Jew with a little money in the bank, enough for a house. The real estate market became so active that even sub-agents could make a great deal of money.

During the war the number of Jewish homeowners and landlords increased rapidly. Some Jewish construction workers or carpenters became building contractors who erected large commercial buildings and residential housing.

Among the new neighbourhoods built at that time was the Papineau district. The construction in Papineau was regarded as an entirely Jewish undertaking. Jews who worked for the CPR far from the centre of the city, and small businessmen such as fruit and junk peddlers, bought lots in Papineau where, with their own hands, they built small houses. These little houses looked like the cottages in their home towns of Russia and Rumania.

Every Sunday many Jews would drive out to Papineau to spend the day at a picnic on one of the empty fields and watch how Jews built their own little houses with genuine enthusiasm and excitement. The best tradesmen were the C.P.R. workers who could work faster and more systematically. They also built barns for cows in the hope that Jews in Papineau would drink milk from their own cows and eat the eggs of their own chickens.

At the time a campaign was conducted among the tailors and cloakmakers urging them to leave their flats in the city and move to Papineau where they could live in their own homes and feed their children fresh milk and fresh eggs every day. Some tailors did in fact move to Papineau, but very few. For the majority of tailors and cloakmakers such a move was far too difficult.

Transition

DURING THE WAR, many tailors and cloakmakers wanted to leave the sweatshops. In 1916 and 1917 relations between the tailors and their employers deteriorated. In 1917 a large number of tailors were impoverished by a bitter general strike which lasted for weeks. Their families found themselves destitute. Many tailors then began to think seriously of abandoning their trade. A large number left to work in the munitions factories, but their main ambition was to acquire a small business such as a grocery, a candy store, a newsstand, or a valet stand to mend and press used clothing. In fact, many tailors and cloakmakers did acquire small businesses, some of which grew into large businesses. The size of the Jewish middle class was thereby increased.

Important changes also came about in the social and cultural spheres. During the war Jews became more interested in community work, particularly in activities concerning world Jewry. Every Jew felt and understood that the war had completely changed the face of Europe and totally transformed Jewish life on the European continent.

In 1917 and 1918 the borders of the Eastern European countries were fundamentally altered. These changes had a profound impact on the political, social, and cultural life of European Jewry, especially when Poland and Lithuania became independent with sharply defined boundaries. The large Russian Jewish community, with its important cultural and religious centres was divided.

In Russia, Jewish life was transformed not only on a material level, but also intellectually and ideologically. This transformation had an impact on many Jewish organizations in Montreal, especially the workers' organizations and unions. Ideological disputes and friction arose between those members who welcomed the changes and those who considered them dangerous.

With regard to culture, the war had the effect of giving Jewish themes a more prominent place in Jewish literature, replacing the class themes which had predominated during the immigrant period. As soon as the war was over, writers, poets, rabbis, devotees of culture, famous pedagogues and artists began arriving from Europe. Their influence was soon felt. Jewish newspapers grew thicker in size and richer in content. New York publishing companies began to produce numerous volumes of fiction, poetry, history, cultural studies, and neo-Hasidism. These books were available in the four Jewish bookstores in the Jewish neighbourhood on Main Street.

During World War I progress was made in the field of religious education. In 1917 the Talmud Torahs were united under one administration with Samuel Weiner as the first president of the united Talmud Torahs. Through the initiative of Isaac Gold, an important member of the Jewish Board of Education, the Bialik School was founded in the north end of the city with Y. B. Cohen as its principal.

Classes in Gemara were already in existence. The first yeshiva in Montreal had opened in a house on Henri Julien near St. Louis Park. Rabbi Bunim Yelin was the head of the yeshiva. Prior to that Rev. H. Kruger and Rabbi Y. M. Margoles had taught little boys Gemara in the Beys Yosef veShmuel Synagogue. Among the more famous Talmud Torah teachers were H. Losinsky, M. Rozovich, and M. Magid, the present principal of the Talmud Torah.

Interest in Jewish education continued to grow. A few years later H. Wolofsky became the president of the Talmud Torah Building Fund for the construction of the new building on St. Joseph Boulevard. However, the financial problems of Talmud Torah remained pressing, and from time to time the teachers would protest that their salaries were not being paid on time. The financial situation finally stabilized when Lazarus Phillips, Q. C.,[247] Abe Bronfman, and Ben Beutel, the current president, became active in the Talmud Torah's annual fund-raising campaign.

The Canadian Jewish Congress

THE FIRST SESSION of the Canadian Jewish Congress took place in March of 1919. The campaign for a congress had begun several years earlier. However, it took a long time to convince certain segments of the Jewish population that it was necessary to have an organization like the Congress to unite all shades and stripes of Jews so that Jewish representatives could speak to the world on behalf of the entire people.

Opponents of the Congress presented various arguments. Wealthy Jews said that a Jewish Congress would be interpreted by non-Jews as Jewish citizens wanting to separate themselves from the general population by building a city within a city. The general Zionists argued that a Jewish Congress would include anti-Zionist groups thereby revealing to the world that Jews were not united in their demand for a homeland in Palestine. The general socialists believed that a Jewish Congress would be preoccupied with Zionism and Jewish community politics. They were not interested. The Jewish question, they maintained, would be settled once the problems of the workers of the world were solved.

The supporters of the Congress struggled hard to break the opposition and were finally successful. The following circumstances played a part. Affluent Jews saw the world rapidly changing as socialist and labour parties made gains in all countries. It had become necessary to join forces with the poorer segments of society and share with them control over Jewish community work. The general Zionists came to the conclusion that anti-Zionist groups could do less harm within Congress, where they would be subject to a certain amount of discipline, than if they were to remain independent on the outside. Left-wing socialists, having witnessed the slaughter of Jews in Poland and the Ukraine, even after the great victories of the socialist and labour parties, recognized that a unique Jewish problem did in fact exist, which was not part and parcel of general working-class problems.

The first session of the Congress was inaugurated at the Monument National Theatre. On the stage decorated with Jewish flags sat ten rabbis.

Rabbi Zvi Cohen opened the meeting with a prayer. Lyon Cohen welcomed the 210 delegates and many guests from all over the country, expressing his great pleasure that for the first time Jews of all affiliations and outlooks had gathered in the Jewish national interest.

Among the speakers at the first meeting were Rabbi Dr. H. Abramowitz, Reuben Brainin, Clarence de Sola, Peter Bercovitch, and Dr. Chaim Zhitlovksy. The most dramatic moment came when Clarence de Sola, in the course of his address, revealed that he had received a cable from "reliable sources" in London to the effect that the British government had finalized its plan for an independent Jewish national homeland in Palestine and that the whole matter of Eretz Israel was, for all intents and purposes, already settled.

Dr. Zhitlovsky in his speech requested that Yiddish receive the same status as Hebrew in the Jewish homeland. About Eretz Israel itself he spoke with such optimism, as if he were certain that it already belonged to the Jews and all that remained was to decide which language to speak there.

On the second day the delegates drove to City Hall. There they were officially received by the acting mayor, Col. Creelman. Welcoming the delegates on behalf of the city, Col. Creelman stated that the residents of Montreal were pleased that Jews were able to establish a Jewish homeland in Palestine. For this reception City Hall was decorated with a Jewish flag.

Congress met for three days. Although most of the speeches and lectures were in Yiddish, the proceedings were conducted in three languages. There was a recording secretary for Yiddish, H. Hershman, a second recording secretary for Hebrew, Benjamin Weiner, and a third for English, Y. Wilder. On Monday and Tuesday the sessions were held in Auditorium Hall.

Most of the speeches and discussions had to do with formulating Jewish demands for the Peace Conference at Versailles. Upon the suggestion of H. Wolofsky, a resolution was adopted to send a delegation to Paris, which, together with Jewish delegations from other countries, would present Jewish demands at the Peace Conference. The two main demands were a Jewish homeland in Palestine and equal rights for Jews all over the world.

Key-note addresses were delivered by Dr. Chaim Zhitlovsky and Louis Fitch on the subject of Eretz Israel, by Rabbi Kahanovitch (Winnipeg) on Jewish unity, about the movement for the five-day work week by Rabbi J. Gordon (Toronto), on immigration by S.W. Jacobs, and by S. Belkin on Jewish rights in Canada.

The speech of Rabbi Gordon drew thunderous applause from the socialist delegates. The rabbi had advocated a five-day work week for the purpose of allowing people to rest on Saturday. For the socialists, this coincided with the workers' dream of a forty-hour work week.

On the executive of the Congress were Lyon Cohen, elected as president and H. M. Caiserman, general secretary. In its early years the Congress generated much excitement which later waned. Most delegates at the first session were under the impression that the Congress was needed for the sole purpose of presenting Jewish demands at the Peace Conference.

For a number of years the Congress was completely inactive. But the entire time the general secretary, H.M. Caiserman, stood at the helm and steered the Congress ship, even when the ship was empty. For many years Congress consisted of a desk in a corner of the Baron de Hirsch Institute where the general secretary was constantly working on Congress business, which involved monitoring anti-Semitic incidents in Canada, and occasionally responding to one or another anti-Semite in the name of the Jewish community.

Although the Congress was a small institution compared to today, it always enjoyed recognition by governments and various Christian organizations as the body authorized to speak on behalf of Canadian Jewry. The Congress was always the address of Canadian Jews. In the Nazi period, the Congress with its limited apparatus led an effective campaign for a boycott of German goods and at the same time directed a defensive campaign against anti-Semitic groups in Canada.

With the rise of Hitler, the Jewish masses paid more attention to the Congress. Once more people became aware of the importance of this national Jewish organization. The Canadian Jewish Congress again became an active national organization when Samuel Bronfman took over the leadership as president, and later when Saul Hayes became the executive director.

Protest and Mourning

THE YEAR 1919 began with the Peace Conference in Paris and with great expectations for the smaller and weaker nations. But for the Jews of Poland and the Ukraine it was a year of blood and tears. For its Jewish inhabitants, Poland became a place of poverty, deprivation, and anti-Semitism.

The nationalistic leaders of the new Poland did not want to permit Jews to occupy key positions in the Polish economy, especially in the area of commerce and finance. From the very outset rampant economic and political anti-Semitism manifested itself in pogroms against the Jews and in the imposition of high taxes on Jewish businesses.

Montreal Jews with relatives in Poland were extremely worried. Jews who had come from Russia were also fearful for their families because of the pogroms being perpetrated by anti-Soviet bands, particularly in the Ukraine. In 1919 the Jews of Montreal spent many hours in protest and mourning. The Jewish alderman Leon V. Jacobs, introduced a protest resolution against Poland in the Montreal City Hall which passed unanimously.

In the Parliament of Canada, S.W. Jacobs, the Jewish member, condemned the Polish government for allowing pogroms against Jews, and a Christian member of Parliament requested that Canada break off trade relations with Poland. In response, the Minister of Justice declared that the League of Nations could be counted upon to protect the Jews of Poland. The League of Nations, however, did nothing.

The Polish government defended its actions by claiming that it was persecuting Bolsheviks, not Jews. In Vilna, Poles shot the Jewish writer A. Veiter on the pretext that he was a Bolshevik. In Pinsk, thirty-three Zionists were shot on the same day that they were arrested at a meeting. These Zionists were also declared to be Bolsheviks. To a large extent, public opinion in Canada and the United States believed the Poles.

In May of 1919 at the Monument National Theatre, the Jews of Montreal protested and wept at a mass meeting of protest and mourning against the persecution of Jews in Poland. Rabbi Zvi Cohen, Louis Fitch, H. M. Caiserman, S.W. Jacobs and H. Barsky were the speakers. They condemned the Polish government for squandering its newly won freedom by instigating pogroms against Jews, and warned the Polish rulers, that they would lose their power over the Polish people if they continued to oppress weak minorities in their country.

As for the pogroms in the Ukraine, there was no one against whom to protest. The bands who perpetrated the pogroms had no diplomatic relations with Canada or England. All one could do was grieve and weep.

In November of 1919 the Jews of Montreal held a procession of mourning and a demonstration on the streets of the city. This was the largest memorial procession ever to have taken place in Montreal. Thirty thousand Jews participated in this procession led by an orchestra playing sombre funeral marches.

The marchers made a powerful impact. At the head of the procession were the founders of the Canadian Jewish Congress—Lyon Cohen, S. W. Jacobs, H. M. Caiserman, and H. Wolofsky. Next came the city's rabbis. Behind the rabbis marched 5,000 Jewish school children, followed by Jewish soldiers who were veterans of the war. After them came members of unions, fraternal organizations and societies, and finally non-affiliated Jews, both men and women. The marchers were wearing black armbands.

The procession filed through the main streets of the city, from Main Street near Duluth, down to St. James Street, along St. James past the offices of *La Presse* and the *Star* and the large financial institutions to Inspector Street. From there it followed Craig Street as far as Beaver Hall Hill, up the mountain to Phillips Square and to St. Catherine Street, then along St. Catherine to Main Street and the Monument National Theatre. In the theatre the demonstration ended with a huge mass meeting.

At the mass meeting women wept aloud, while men sobbed quietly. Rabbi Zvi Cohen, Lyon Cohen, S. W. Jacobs, Louis Fitch, H. M. Caiserman, S. Belkin and H. Barsky addressed the crowd. They sharply criticized the representatives of the great powers who were working on world peace in Versailles and warned that if they continued to ignore the widespread slaughter of Jews, the peace they were carefully constructing would collapse, unleashing a second world war much more devastating than the first.

The non-Jewish press showed little interest in the pogroms in Poland and the Ukraine. The articles about the Ukraine reported that a civil war was being waged between the Bolsheviks and the anti-Bolshevik armies. For the most part, their sympathies did not lie with the Bolsheviks.

Poland was depicted in the non-Jewish newspapers as a democratic country struggling valiantly against Bolshevik influences. The newspapers often printed letters from Polish Canadians accusing American Jews of fabricating slanderous lies about the new Poland in order to discredit Poland in the eyes of the West. Only the openly liberal newspapers, of which there were very few, came out in defense of the Jews.

In Montreal Polish and Ukrainian Jews became active in providing aid to the suffering Jews of Poland and the Ukraine. They founded *landsmanshaften*, fraternal organizations, devoted to relief work.

The Association of Ukrainian Jews collected used clothing and medicines, sending S. Belkin as its representative to the Ukraine to organize their distribution. Collecting clothing for the Ukrainian Jews became the work of the entire Jewish community of Canada. The Jewish newspapers referred to the tragedy of the Ukrainian Jews as the third *khurbn* or catastrophe, equal to the destruction of the first and second Temples in Jerusalem. At the time no one could have imagined that approximately twenty-five years later a much greater catastrophe would take place in Europe.

The Association of Polish Jews was also dedicated to political work. It made every effort to convince the Canadian government to exert pressure on the Polish regime to improve its treatment of Polish Jews.

In the Ukraine the situation normalized when the Soviet regime suppressed the groups which had perpetrated pogroms. The Association of Ukrainian Jews then ceased its activities. Thereafter mainly radical pro-Soviet Jews took an interest in the economic and social life of Soviet Jewry. They founded ICOR, an organization,[248] which assisted Russian Jews to settle in agricultural colonies. Among the original active members of ICOR in Montreal were Israel Hirshbein and Shlomo Kach. At the same time the American Jewish Joint Agricultural Corporation or Agro-Joint[249] was very active in helping to resettle Soviet Jews on the land. Jewish colonies in the Ukraine and the Crimea were organized with the assistance of American and Canadian Jews.

Festival of the Restoration

In 1919 the Jews of Montreal marched in the streets in a procession of mourning. One year later, in 1920, they held a festive parade of redemption (*geulah* parade).

In 1920 the mood was considerably brighter than the year before when every day the Jewish newspapers had been full of tragic news about pogroms against the Jews of the Ukraine. In 1919 the danger loomed that the perpetrators of these pogroms would prevail, drowning Russian Jewry in blood. In its struggle against the White Guards, the Soviet regime had defeated and suppressed the Ukrainian bands, and by 1920 the pogroms had stopped.

In April, 1920, at a conference in San Remo, Italy, the world powers concluded a peace treaty with Turkey. The treaty incorporated the Balfour Declaration with regard to a Jewish National Home in Palestine under a British mandate. This was the great historical event of the year joyfully celebrated in all the large centres of Canada and the United States with pomp and ceremony.

A special holiday edition of the *Keneder Adler* was printed in Montreal in several colours which issued a call to all Jews to fly Jewish and Canadian flags from their homes and stores. Tuesday, the fourth of May, was proclaimed a holiday, and Jewish flags fluttered above the houses in all the streets of the Jewish quarter.

A great parade of redemption was held which included automobiles. Five hundred cars decorated with Jewish and Canadian flags left Fletcher's Field at seven o' clock in the evening. They continued on to Laurier, crossed Main Street, drove down to St. Catherine, west to Guy Street, through Sherbrooke to Park Avenue, took Prince Arthur to St. Urbain Street and went up to the arena on Mount Royal between Clark and St. Urbain.

In the arena 10,000 Jews applauded eagerly as several speakers addressed eloquent words of praise and gratitude to England for bestowing the status of a nation upon the Jewish people and for bringing an end to Jewish exile. The chairman was Dr. Friedman. Lyon Cohen thanked England in the name of the Canadian Jewish Congress, Louis Fitch on behalf of the Zionist

The Festival of the Restoration

Wednesday, May the Fifth

has been proclaimed by the

Executive Committee of the Canadian Zionist Federation

— as a —

NATIONAL HOLIDAY

to celebrate the granting by the San Remo
Supreme Council of the Mandate to
Great Britain for Palestine.   ::   ::

Let us celebrate the beginning of our
Restoration in a worthy manner.

LET EVERY JEWISH HOME AND PLACE OF
BUSINESS BE DECORATED WITH JEWISH AND
BRITISH FLAGS.

LET IT BE A GENERAL FESTIVAL—NOT A
FESTIVAL OF ANY PARTICULAR CLASS—FOR
WE MUST SHOW THAT THIS GREAT HISTORI-
CAL MOMENT HAS UNITED ALL JEWRY INTO
ONE PEOPLE.

We have mourned and wept throughout
the centuries---we must now rejoice and
celebrate our Restoration.   ::   ::

Federation of Zionist Societies of Canada, Inc.
MONTREAL.

Announcement, *Canadian Jewish Chronicle*, April 30, 1920.
Five hundred cars decorated with Jewish and Canadian flags left
Fletcher's Field at seven o'clock in the evening to celebrate
the ratification of the Balfour Declaration. The parade ended at
the Mount Royal arena which was packed with a jubilant crowd of 10,000.

Federation, H.M. Caiserman and S. Belkin on behalf of the Labour Zionists. An orchestra played between the speeches and a choir of cantors performed songs which symbolized the return to Zion.

Before the Balfour Declaration was ratified in San Remo, the news from Palestine had been far from encouraging. Frequent clashes between Arabs and Jewish colonists had been reported. The Jews, apparently receiving little support from the British authorities, were organizing themselves in self-defence. Jabotinsky[250] was arrested on the same day as the Balfour Declaration was endorsed in San Remo, and sentenced to fifteen years in prison. In many cities in America and England, and also in Montreal, Jews protested. Jabotinsky's sentence was reduced. Jews hoped that the British crackdown was only temporary and that a new epoch was about to begin, the epoch of Jewish statehood in Eretz Israel. Rumours circulated that London had great plans for the Jews, including a Jewish Governor-General. Herbert Samuel, a Jew who attended synagogue every Saturday, was to be the representative of the King.

The Jewish papers in the days following San Remo carried many redemption stories. There were reports about Zionist parades in all the large urban centres of the United States. On the front page of the *Keneder Adler* in capital letters was a lengthy cable from England which described how Dr. Chaim Weizmann and Nahum Sokolov were received in London with a big parade "like victorious statesmen" upon their return from San Remo. During a large London redemption celebration Max Nordau passionately declared: "England has fulfilled its duty toward Eretz Israel. It is now the turn of the Jews."

In those days it seemed that England was already on side. All that remained was to win over certain Jewish groups such as extremely wealthy Jews, who were assimilationist, and left-wing Jews, who were internationalist. The Zionist leaders were concerned about the opposition of these groups.

In 1920 the Jews of Montreal began for the first time to donate large amounts of money for overseas relief. Eastern Europe was now accessible to Jewish relief efforts and the appeals for help came from many Jewish communities.

For the first time a million-dollar campaign was proclaimed in Montreal for overseas relief. The campaign was launched at a large mass meeting in the Gayety Theatre. An important guest arrived from New York for this meeting—Louis Marshall. Marshall was then the acknowledged leader of American Jewry, a leading figure among the Jewish delegates who had attended the peace conference in Versailles. Other speakers at the mass meeting were Lyon Cohen, Sir Mortimer B. Davis, Maxwell Goldstein, and Marcus Sperber. In this campaign Montreal Jews of all political and religious persuasions participated. Uptowners and downtowners were united.

The first large fundraising campaign was well-organized. Weeks before it began, conferences and consultations among the uptowners and downtowners took place to ensure that the entire amount of one million dollars would be collected. This, however, turned out to be difficult. The full amount was not obtained on time and the campaign had to be extended. Nevertheless, this was the beginning of large-scale fundraising.

One year later, in 1921, at a Zionist conference in Montreal, the Zionist Organization also proclaimed a million-dollar campaign for its foundation fund, the *Keren Hayesod*. James Rothschild[251] was the guest of honour at this convention. In that year Jews also began to donate large sums of money for Eretz Israel.

The New Immigrants

In 1920 Jewish immigrants from Europe once more began to arrive in Canada. They were quite different from those who had immigrated prior to the war. Many of the new immigrants were received by well-to-do relatives. They were able to find lighter work, a good number becoming white collar workers.

Those who decided to go into the clothing trades did not have to work long hours in sweatshops. In fact, sweatshops by that time had almost ceased to exist. In the war years the Tailors' and Cloakmakers' Unions had fought successfully for improved working conditions. In 1919 the tailors began to work only forty-four hours a week. In the few years prior to 1920 large modern ten-storey buildings were erected in the garment district. Most of the tailoring, cloak and dress shops moved into them. Dress shops came into existence right after the war.

At the same time, the fur trade began to flourish. During the war, when more people earned a good living, more women began to wear fur coats. The fur industry was developed by Jews, and to this day remains a "Jewish" industry.

The new immigrants of the post-war period adapted more quickly to the life of the community. As a matter of fact, they found a much better organized Jewish community in Montreal. Philanthropic, political, and cultural organizations and institutions were already in place. Since 1916 most philanthropic organizations had been united under the Federation of Jewish Philanthropies.[252] There was also a large Jewish library and a sizeable group of intellectuals, writers, and poets. Zionist and other Jewish nationalist organizations were very active.

Among the new immigrants were Jewish writers, poets, artists, rabbis, teachers and even Hasidic rabbis. An entirely different atmosphere prevailed, unlike that prior to 1914 when most newly arrived immigrants were poor people who came for the sole purpose of working to earn a livelihood. The majority of the new immigrants had left Europe to escape the revolutionary and counter-revolutionary uncertainty sweeping Russia, and on account of the political and economic anti-Semitism rampant in Poland.

In 1920, when a new wave of Jewish immigration began to flow into Canada, the Jewish Immigrant Aid Society was organized. Its founding took place at a conference at the Baron de Hirsch Institute, convened on the initiative of the Canadian Jewish Congress, with the cooperation of the various fraternal organizations. Its first executive consisted of Louis Fitch as president, L. Coviensky as vice-president, Rabbi Zvi Cohen as treasurer, and H. M. Caiserman as secretary.

Art Needle Shop, 3968 St. Lawrence Blvd., 1925.
Esther Reva Fineberg opened this hand embroidery
shop in 1918.
Archives of Ontario F1405-23-103, MSR8427 #5

Immigrant Orphans

IN 1920 A CAMPAIGN was launched in Montreal to bring immigrant orphans from the Ukraine, children who had lost their parents in the bloody pogroms of 1919. Mrs. Lillian Freiman of Ottawa took charge of this project. She convened a conference in Ottawa of Jewish community leaders where it was decided to bring over as many orphans as possible. Mrs. Freiman travelled to a number of cities in Canada to make an appeal on behalf of the Ukrainian orphans. Everywhere the response of the Jews was heartfelt. Money was donated and people registered to become "parents" and adopt orphaned children upon their arrival.

A special messenger, H. Hershman, was sent to the Ukraine to organize the adoptions and gather together the children. Hershman assembled 150 children who had been orphaned by the pogroms, and arrived with them in Antwerp. Mrs. Freiman went to Antwerp to meet the children and bring them to Canada.

These orphans were among the first post-war immigrants. A record of them is kept to this day. Among them are well-to-do businessmen and successful professionals. A few served in the Canadian armed forces and distinguished themselves in World War II.

Bringing the orphans from the Ukraine was one of the largest relief efforts carried out by the Jews of Canada following the 1914 war.

Farewell to Yesterday

POST-WAR IMMIGRANTS, as I have said earlier, encountered conditions in Canada unlike those experienced by the immigrants who had arrived prior to 1914. The end of the war closed a long chapter of Jewish life in Europe. The "yesterday" chapter of modern Jewish history was over.

After the war a new epoch began with high hopes and expectations for the Jews of Europe. It ended in the most catastrophic tragedy in Jewish history. It was a very short and bloody chapter.

In the post-war years, it appeared as though a more prosperous and just world was being created in which Jews would be treated as equal citizens in all the countries of Europe. At the same time a moderate flow of immigration to Palestine would slowly but surely help to establish the Jewish national homeland.

These hopes were based on the apparent strength of the socialists and liberals at the time. But socialists and liberals were gradually forced out of their positions of influence in European governments to be replaced by reactionary and unscrupulous statesmen. For the Jews of Europe the atmosphere became more and more oppressive. With the advent of Nazism, the fate of the Jews of Europe was sealed.

At the same time, the Jews of Canada and the United States were experiencing a period of growth and renewal in all fields. Large Jewish communities built on the American continent were the successors of the declining Jewish communities in Europe. The foundations of the flourishing Jewish community of Montreal, one of the largest in North America, with its many great cultural and philanthropic institutions, were laid by the pioneers of yesterday.

It was the immigrant Jews in the period before 1914 who prepared the soil on which new Jewish life and an important Jewish community could grow and prosper. The pioneers of yesterday were the first builders of Jewish life in Canada.

Israel Medres in Outremont, Quebec, shortly before
his death in 1964.
Photo by Abe Madras.

Translator's Notes — Introduction

[1] Between December 1, 1946 and June 25, 1947

[2] Literally "Canadian Eagle." In English the *Eagle* was identified as a "Jewish Daily" and in Yiddish as a "Canadian" newspaper.

[3] Rosenberg, Louis, *Canada's Jews: A Social and Economic Study of the Jews in Canada*, edited by Morton Weinfield, pages 150 and 308, and Census of Canada, 1901, 1911, and 1921

[4] Incidentally, when one reads the chapter headings and sub-headings in *World of Our Fathers*, the widely acclaimed study by Irving Howe published in 1976 about the life of the Eastern European Jewish immigrants in New York, the similarity to those in *Montreal of Yesterday* is striking.

[5] In his book, *My Lexicon (Pen portraits of Jewish Writers and Artists in the Americas and other Countries)*, Tel Aviv: I.L. Peretz Publishing House, 1982, page 87

[6] Z.Y. Gitelman, *Jewish Nationality and Soviet Politics*, Princeton: Princeton University Press, 1972, page 20.

[7] J. Fishman, ed., *Studies in Modern Jewish Social History*, New York: Ktav Publishing House, 1972, pages 100-2

[8] H. Nevinson, *The Dawn in Russia*, page 219; O.O. Gruzenberg, *Vchera*, Paris, 1938, pages 130-2

[9] S.M. Dubnow, *History of the Jews in Russia and Poland*, v.3, page 41

[10] Dubnow, S. *Nationalism and History*, New York: Meridian Books, 1961, page 20; S. Levin, *Forward From Exile*, Philadelphia: The Jewish Publication Society, 1967, page 402

[11] S. Harcave, "The Jews in the First Russian Election," *American and East European Review*, v.9, 1950, page 36

[12] For example in the *New York Times*, May 27, 1906 and on page 48 of *Montreal of Yesterday*. Elected to the Duma were twelve Jews, among them Shmaryahu Levin whom Medres writes about in the book.

[13] See chapter on Canada, page 76ff.

[14] *Encyclopedia Judaica*, vol. 13, page 656 ff.

[15] Also the birthplace of the well-known Yiddish theatre critic Alexander Mukdoni (1878-1958), pseudonym of Alexander Cappell, who in the United States wrote for the *Morgn Zhurnal*.

[16] *Encyclopedia Judaica*, volume 14, page 58

[17] *Encyclopedia Judaica*, volume 14, page 58

[18] Israel and Sophie Medres had four children. Samuel Madras, born in 1915, who became Dean of Science at Sir George Williams University, Montreal; Abraham Madras (1917-1998) who was chairman of the Joint Committee of the

Men's and Boys' Clothing Industry of the Province of Quebec; Anne Medres Glass (1919-1982) who taught the first classes in Yiddish language and literature at the University of Toronto; and Philip Madras, born 1921, chartered accountant, Montreal.

[19] In 1928 Israel Medres applied to the Canadian authorities for permission to bring over a 22-year-old brother from Baranovichi, then in Poland, and was rejected.

[20] See, for example, Melech Ravitch, op.cit., 1980, pp.87-88.

[21] See Chaim Spilberg and Yaacov Zipper, editors, *Canadian Jewish Anthology*, Montreal: Canadian Jewish Congress, 1982.

[22] *Le Montréal juif d'autrefois*, Sillery, Quebec: Les Éditions de Septentrion, 1997.

[23] The French version of *Montreal of Yesterday* was required reading in a course on Canadian Jewish literature at the Université de Montréal in 1999.

[24] For example, Jacques Lacoursière, *Histoire Populaire du Québec*, volume 4, Sillery, Quebec: Les Éditions de Septentrion, 1997: Bernard Dansereau, "La Place des travailleurs juifs dans le mouvement ouvrier Québécois au début du XXe Siècle," unpublished paper delivered at a conference entitled "Les rélations judéo-Québécoises: identités et perceptions mutuelles," Montreal, March 25, 1999.

[25] See the following chapters: Sick Benefit Societies, Politics and Citizenship, Academic Anti-Semitism, The Attack on the Talmud, The Historic Decision, and the obituaries in the *Keneder Adler*, August 5, 1964.

Translator's Notes — All Chapters

[1] *Montreal of Yesterday* was published in 1947.

[2] Today René-Lévesque Boulevard. At the beginning of the 20th century Dorchester Street was only a two-lane street.

[3] This term refers to people who come from the same town in the old country. Singular is *landsman*.

[4] Now St. Antoine Street.

[5] Today Jeanne-Mance Street.

[6] This street was shortened to allow for the construction of the Guy Favreau Building, as was Chénéville Street.

[7] Today De Bullion Street.

[8] This refers to Victoria Square which was the site of a hay market up to the middle of the 19th century.

[9] On February 21, 1936, I. Medres wrote in the *Canadian Jewish Chronicle*: "In Dupré Lane the homes were demolished and a big brewery built in their place. On St. Maurice Street . . . two or three Jewish grocery stores, a few Jewish butcher shops and a big tailoring shop . . . have been torn down and replaced by factories or garages."

[10] Today Viger Avenue.

[11] Notre Dame Street, at the time one of the most important shopping districts of Montreal, was full of Jewish stores. At the corner of Notre Dame and McGill Street stood Workman's Store, one of the most popular clothing stores in the city. From there to the end of Notre Dame Street West one found stores selling clothing, shoes, furniture, dry goods, dresses, and second-hand goods. There were also Jewish groceries. The junk and rag businesses were concentrated in the "Griffintown" section, from Notre Dame Street to the Canal and from McCord to McGill street. See I. Medres, in the *Canadian Jewish Chronicle*, February 21, 1936, page 5

[12] See I. Medres, in the *Canadian Jewish Chronicle*, February 21, 1936, page 5.

[13] *Klapper* is literally "one who knocks", someone who sold door to door.

[14] A custom-peddler, or customer peddler, was a peddler who had a regular route and regular clientele.

[15] Baron Maurice de Hirsch (1831-1896) Jewish philanthropist, born in Munich, who founded the Jewish Colonization Association (ICA) to help the Jews of Russia settle in agricultural colonies in Argentina and elsewhere.

[16] The building was situated on Bleury Street, at the corner of de Maisonneuve, on the site of the present Place-des-Arts métro station.

[17] Israel Zangwill (1864-1926), British Jewish writer, famous for his novels about Jewish life in London.

[18] Harris Vineberg (1855-1942) emigrated to Montreal from Lithuania in 1872, and became the first president of the Baron de Hirsch Institute in 1888.

Alliance Israelite universelle is a Jewish organization founded in 1860 in Paris to defend civil and religious liberties. It estabished Jewish schools throughout the Balkans, Asia, North Africa, and the Middle East.

[19] (1834-1914)

[20] (1858-1920). From an illustrious Sephardic family which settled in Montreal in the mid-19th century, he served as Belgian consul in Montreal from 1904-1920. See chapter on Zionist politics, page 110ff.

[21] (1844-1914). Born in Poland, emigrated to Canada in 1869, settled in Montreal in 1883. A prominent businessman, he was one of the foremost leaders of the Montreal Jewish community at the turn of the century.

[22] (1868-1937). Clothing manufacturer, he owned Freedman and Company, one of the largest and most successful clothing firms. He was one of the founders of the *Jewish Times*, the first Jewish periodical in Canada, and president of the Baron de Hirsch Institute from 1908 to 1912. In 1919, he became the first president of the Canadian Jewish Congress.

[23] Zvi Hirsch Cohen (1862-1950). Having arrived from Eastern Europe in 1889, he became the unofficial chief rabbi of Montreal. For many years he was the chairman of the Council of Orthodox Rabbis of Montreal.

[24] (1860-1936). Settled in Montreal in 1893. From 1910 he was the head of the legal claims department of the Baron de Hirsch Institute.

[25] This word was incorporated into Yiddish to mean the money a worker received

from his or her employer and not the day it was paid.

[26] The *Canadian Jewish Chronicle*, February 21, 1936, "Montreal, Yesterday, Today" by I. Medres, translated by Eli M. Berger. "The Jewish immigrant somehow or other, did not feel so very much at home in the local *shul*. The rules, printed and posted where you saw them as soon as you entered, seemed foreign to him. 'Talking during service is not permitted. Walking back and forth is prohibited. Keep your seat. The *talith* is not to be removed until after *oleynu*. Putting the talith over your head and swaying to and fro is not permitted.'"

[27] (1874-1949). American rabbi and Zionist leader.

[28] Harry Joshua Stern (1892-1984) Born in Lithuania, educated in the U.S., and from 1927 the rabbi of the Temple Emanu-El in Montreal.

[29] Dr. Herman Abramowitz (1880-1947) Born in Russia, educated in the U.S. before becoming rabbi of the Sha'ar Hashomayim Synagogue in 1903.

[30] Today de Maisonneuve Boulevard.

[31] Both a few kilometres east of St. Jerome.

[32] Zigmond Fineberg (1863-1967) Born in Poland, emigrated to Montreal in 1887 where he became involved in business and real estate. In 1911 he founded the Hebrew Free Loan Association which by 1923 had lent up to $100,000 interest-free.

[33] The Labour Temple was situated on La Gauchetière Street just east of St. Lawrence Boulevard and Prince Arthur Hall was on the north side of Prince Arthur between St. Dominique and Coloniale.

[34] See below, notes 51, 53, and 56.

[35] "Waist" in those days meant blouse.

[36] Socialist-anarchist newspaper first published in New York in 1890.

[37] (1847-1920). American Jewish financier and philanthropist.

[38] See Alexander Whyte Wright, *Report Upon the Sweating System in Canada*, Secretary of State, Sesssional Papers, 1896, vol. 29, no. 61, and quoted in the Canadian Jewish Archives New Series, No. 9 "Our Forerunners – At Work," 1978.

[39] Hirsch Hershman (1876-1955) immigrated to Montreal in 1902 from Bukovina (Rumania). One of the founders of the Jewish Public Library in 1914 and the Peretz School, he was active all his life in the Montreal Yiddish literary scene.

[40] The pseudonym of Nahum Meyer Shaikevich (1849-1905), Russian-born Yiddish novelist and playwright who emigrated to the United States in 1880. Wrote numerous popular novels and plays where good always triumphed over evil.

[41] A. Tannenbaum (1848-1913), one of the most prolific and popular of the Yiddish novelists who often wrote in the manner of Jules Verne.

[42] Oyzer Blaustein (1898-1940) and Moishe Seifert (1851-1922) were also popular Yiddish writers.

[43] Captain Alfred Dreyfus (1859-1935), French officer of Jewish descent. While a member of the French general staff, he was condemned as a spy and imprisoned. He was later acquitted of the charge and reinstated to the army. The case divided all of France into two opposing camps, and the anti-Semitism it unleashed

contributed to the popularity of the Zionist ideal.

[44] Bohdan Chmielnicki (or Khmelnitsky) (1593-1657) Cossack leader who headed the revolt of the Cossack and Ukrainian masses against the Polish landowners in 1648 which resulted in the annihilation of hundreds of Jewish communities and the murder of hundreds of thousands of Jews.

[45] Gershom BenYehudah (965-1028), one of the first commentators on the Talmud, was known for his legal decisions including bans on polygamy, divorcing a woman without her consent, reading letters directed to others, cutting pages out of books, and mocking converts who returned to Judaism.

[46] (1626-1676). A false messiah whose fame spread throughout the Jewish world beginning in 1665 and sharply divided the rabbis of Europe.

[47] Simon Bar Kokhba, died 135 C.E. Leader of the revolt of the Jews (131-135) against the Romans.

[48] (1856-1933). Yiddish poet and essayist, who emigrated to the United States in 1894, and was dedicated to the cause of socialism.

[49] Pseudonym of Israel Zalman Hurwitz (1872-1955), a Yiddish writer born in Byelorussia who settled in New York in 1893 and wrote plays and short stories about the hardships of Jewish life in New York.

[50] Jacob Gordin (1853-1909). Yiddish playwright who settled in the United States in 1891, writing over 80 plays which revolutionized the modern Yiddish theatre. See chapter on the Monument National, page 92, and footnote 162.

[51] Morris Rosenfeld (1862-1923), a Yiddish poet who emigrated from Russia to the United States and became famous for his poems about the workers in the sweatshops.

[52] Leon Kobrin (1862-1946), a novelist and dramatist who immigrated to the United States in 1892. Influenced by Russian literature, he described the Jewish workers in large American cities.

[53] David Edelstadt (1866-1892), a socialist poet who came to the United States in 1882 and joined the anarchist movement. After his death from tuberculosis at 26 he became a legendary figure.

[54] Philip Krantz (1858-1922), Yiddish journalist who came to New York in 1890 where he became prominent in the Yiddish socialist press.

[55] Abraham Liesin (1872-1938), emigrated to the United States in 1894 where he became a Yiddish writer dedicated to the cause of the workers and socialism.

[56] Benjamin Feigenbaum (1860-1932). Born in Warsaw, he emigrated to the United States in 1891 where he became known as a Yiddish writer, orator, and lecturer on socialism and atheism. He wrote for the *Forward*.

[57] Paul Lafargue (1842-1911), French socialist, son-in-law of Karl Marx, was a popularizer of Marxism.

[58] (1835-1917). One of the founders of modern Yiddish literature, known as the grandfather of Yiddish literature.

[59] Pseudonym of Shalom Rabinovich (1859-1916). Born in the Ukraine, he became, with Mendele Mocher Sforim and I.L. Peretz, one of the founders of modern

Yiddish literature.
[60] Isaac Leib Peretz (1852-1915) settled in Warsaw to become of the most influential of the Yiddish writers.
[61] Jacob Dinesohn (1856-1919), a Yiddish writer in Warsaw who wrote a series of popular sentimental novels.
[62] Simon Samuel Frug (1860-1916) was a Russian Jewish writer who described the sufferings of the Jewish people and the yearning for Zion.
[63] In Yiddish described as "silken" from the silk coats (capotes) they would wear.
[64] Sons-in-law supported by their wives' families.
[65] Haskalah, "the enlightenment," referring to the movement whose aim was to spread modern European culture among the Jews of Europe, from about 1750 to 1880.
[66] The first Hebrew newspaper to appear in Russia, founded in 1860.
[67] One of the first Hebrew newspapers in the 19th century, published in Warsaw.
[68] Nahum Sokolov (1859-1936), a Hebrew writer, Zionist, journalist. Editor of Hatsfirah.
[69] Peretz Smolenskin (1840-1885), Hebrew novelist, editor. In his novels, which describe Jewish life in Eastern Europe, he developed a Jewish national theory that opposed religious Orthodoxy and Haskalah.
[70] Abraham Mapu (1808-1867) Hebrew novelist who wrote the first modern novel in Hebrew, Ahavat Zion.
[71] (1831-1892), Hebrew poet, writer, critic. Editor of Hebrew daily Hamelitz. Many of his poems exposed the faults of Jewish society and its leaders, and the position of the poor and the oppressed, especially women.
[72] Asher Ginsberg (1856-1927), Hebrew essayist, thinker and "cultural" Zionist.
[73] Moses Leib Lilienblum (1843-1910), Hebrew writer, critic, political journalist. One of the leaders of the Haskalah in its last period of Chibat Zion, its Zionist phase. Edited the Yiddish journal Kol Mevasser.
[74] (1874-1958). Literary critic, historian, and editor of the major literary periodical HaShiloah. Author of essays on Jewish history and literature and important histories of modern Hebrew literature and the Second Temple Period.
[75] HaShiloah (the name derives from a spring near Jerusalem, Siloam), was a Hebrew monthly which appeared between 1897 and 1926 and was of exceptionally high literary quality.
[76] (1865-1921). Hebrew novelist and thinker who later changed his name to Bin-Gurion.
[77] Isaiah (Domashevitzky) Bershadsky (1871-1908) Hebrew novelist, teacher and journalist. Regarded as the father of the naturalistic school of Hebrew literature.
[78] About Zionist activity in a typical Russian Jewish community.
[79] Mordecai Ze'ev Feierberg (1874-1899) Russian Hebrew author. He wrote essays and several lyrical novels. The best-known is Le'an (Whither). In his novels he expresses the struggle of the Eastern European Jewish youth at the end of the 19th century, disappointed by the Haskalah yet unable to remain within the bounds

of traditional Jewish observance.

[80] (1861-1922). Hebrew and Yiddish author. Wrote satires, critical essays, stories, and poems, and published translations of European literature. He was responsible for freeing Hebrew fiction from the artificial plot characteristic of the *Haskalah* period.

[81]Heinrich Graetz (1817-1891). German historian and Bible scholar who wrote the 11- volume *History of the Jews* (1853-75).

[82]Karl Kautsky (1854-1938) German-Austrian socialist, a prominent figure in the Second International who opposed Bolshevism and Leninism.

[83] Ferdinand Lassalle (1825-1864), Jewish socialist, opponent of Marx, and founder of the first socialist party in Germany.

[84] August Bebel (1840-1913), a founder of the German Social Democratic party and follower of Marx.

[85] (1884-1927). From 1905 until his death he taught Hebrew at the Baron de Hirsch Institute. He translated modern Hebrew literature into Yiddish for the *Keneder Adler.*

[86] Refers to the Depression of 1907-8.

[87] Michael Bakunin (1814-1876). Russian anarchist theoretician who with Marx founded the First International but was expelled by the Marxists in 1872.

[88] Peter Kropotkin (1842-1921). Russian prince and most famous anarchist theoretician who visited Canada in 1897. On his recommendation the Doukhobors were settled in the Canadian prairies in 1898-99.

[89] Jacob ben Wolf Kranz, the "Magid [Preacher] of Dubno)" (c.1740-1804), Lithuanian scholar who travelled widely and gained a reputation as an outstanding preacher. His writings were published posthumously.

[90] 18th century jester in the courts of various leading Hasidic rabbis. His jokes became part of Jewish folklore.

[91] *Keneder Adler* literally means "Canadian Eagle".

[92] Abraham Reisen (1876-1953). One of the most well-known of the Yiddish writers, a poet and writer of short fiction, born in the Ukraine and settled in New York.

[93] Hirsch David Nomberg (1876-1923). Polish Yiddish writer and founder of the Jewish Polish political party, the *Folkisten*, in 1916, which he represented in the Polish parliament.

[94] Sholem Asch (1880-1957). Yiddish novelist and playwright who immigrated from Poland to the United States, and the first Yiddish writer to establish an international reputation.

[95] David Pinski (1872-1959). Yiddish dramatist, novelist and editor whose plays were translated into English and German and produced before non-Jewish audiences in Germany and New York, the city in which he lived from 1899 to 1949 before settling in Israel.

[96] Theodor Herzl (1860-1904). The father of political Zionism, he founded the World Zionist Organization.

[97] Max Nordau (1894-1932). Hungarian-born author and Zionist leader.

[98] See chapter on Baron de Hirsch Institute and note 17.

[99] See chapter on Hebraists and note 72.

[100] See chapter on Hebraists, pages 133, 134, and note 68.

[101] See chapter on Hebraists and note 74.

[102] A Yiddish newspaper published in St. Petersburg.

[103] A daily Yiddish newspaper printed in Warsaw.

[104] See notes 67 and 68.

[105] The Black Hundreds was the popular name of the reactionary Union of the Russian People founded in 1904 which was headed by numerous government and police officials in the Russian Empire and supported by Czar Nicholas II. The Union of the Russian People was responsible for organizing pogroms, disseminating the anti-Semitic *Protocols of the Elders of Zion*, and engineering the Mendel Beilis ritual murder trial in 1913.

[106] V.M. Purishkevich, vice-president of the Union of the Russian People.

[107] P. A. Krushevan (1860-1909), reactionary author and chief instigator of the 1903 Kishinev pogrom. *The Protocols of the Elders of Zion* was first published in Russia in 1903 in *Znamya* (The Banner) which he edited with financial support from the government.

[108] Hirsch Wolofsky (1876-1949). Born in Poland, he arrived in Montreal in 1900 where he became a leader of the Jewish community.

[109] See page 73 and notes 102, 103, and 104.

[110] Paul Nikolayevich Miliukov (1859-1943). Russian historian and leader of the Constitutional Democratic Party.

[111] Vasilii Alekseevich Maklakov (1870-1957). Statesman, lawyer, and member of the central committee of the Consititutional Democratic (Cadet) party, he served as a Cadet deputy in the second, third, and fourth State Dumas.

[112] Fyodor Ismaylovich Roditchev (1856-1933). Cadet deputy in all four Dumas and one of the founders of the Cadet party.

[113] Rabbi Isaac Elhanan Spector (1817-1896). Officiated in various Lithuanian and Byelorussian towns and from 1864 was rabbi in Kovno where he founded the noted Slobodka Yeshiva.

[114] Rabbi Chaim Soloveichik (1853-1918). Taught at the Volozhin Yeshiva and became rabbi of Brest-Litovsk in 1892.

[115] Israel Meir ha-Kohen (1838-1933). Rabbi, Talmudist. Lived in Radun, Lithuania where he wrote influential books on Jewish ethics.

[116] Chanan Jacob Minikes (1867-1932) was the editor and publisher of this popular illustrated magazine (literally "holiday papers") published on Jewish holidays containing works of prose, poetry, science, and history.

[117] Abdul Hamid (1842-1918). Ottoman sultan who in 1908 was forced by the Young Turks to grant a constitution.

[118] (1879-1963). Born in Zhitomir, Ukraine, and emigrated to the U.S. in 1884 where he became a Zionist and one of the first Yiddish journalists. In 1907-1908 he

lived in Montreal where he edited all the first issues of the *Keneder Adler*.
[119] (1877-1942) Born in the Ukraine, member of the Poalei Zion, lived in Montreal from 1902 to 1912.
[120] Abraham Aaron Roback (1890-1965). Born in Poland, came to Montreal in 1892. Studied at McGill and Harvard, and in 1908 became the editor of the *Keneder Adler* and in 1913 the editor of the *Canadian Jewish Chronicle*.
[121] Ezekiel Wortsman (1878-1938) Journalist, theatre critic, Labour Zionist, editor-in-chief of the *Keneder Adler* from July, 1910 to February, 1912.
[122] Benjamin Gutl Sack (1889-1967). Born in Lithuania, came to Montreal in 1905. Historian, journalist, Labour Zionist. In 1945 his *History of the Jews in Canada* was published in English translation. A second volume in English translation, *Canadian Jews–Early in this Century*, was published in 1975.
[123] Shmuel Talpis (1877-1951). Prolific writer in Hebrew and Yiddish. Born in Lithuania and studied at the Telz Yeshiva. In 1894 he came to Montreal, wrote for the *Keneder Adler* from 1908. Community activist and Labour Zionist.
[124] Isaac Yampolsky. Born in the Ukraine in 1874. Journalist, author. Wrote for the *Keneder Adler* from 1908 to 1911 when he left for New York.
[125] (1871-1947) Born in Podolia. Lived in Montreal from 1909 to 1942. Considered the father of Canadian Yiddish literature. Founder of the Association of Yiddish Writers. Contributor to the *Keneder Adler*.
[126] Shlomo Chaim Shneur (1884-1958). Born in Vilna, fled for political reasons in 1905. Labour Zionist, community activist, journalist and historian.
[127] Zushe Kornblitt (1872-1929). Emigrated to the U.S. in 1892 from Volhynia, one of the first contributors to the *Forward*. Came to Montreal, and from 1910 to 1913 was news editor of the *Keneder Adler*.
[128] (1886-1966). Yiddish author, playwright, novelist. Lived in Montreal from 1905 to 1925 and wrote for the *Keneder Adler*.
[129] Small town in Byelorussia. Its yeshiva, founded in the 19th century, was famous for its teaching methods and opposition to Hasidism.
[130] Small town in Lithuania. Its yeshiva flourished from 1881 and after the Great War relocated to Cleveland.
[131] Suburb of Kovno, Lithuania. Its yeshiva, founded in 1881, was conducted in the spirit of the *Musar* movement which emphasized the study of traditional ethical literature (*musar*) and moral self-criticism.
[132] Famous yeshiva founded in the town of Mir, Byelorussia. Its students escaped in World War II to Shanghai, China.
[133] (1848-1931). American merchant and philanthropist of German origin.
[134] (1856-1929). American lawyer and community leader of German origin, president of the American Jewish Congress 1912-1929.
[135] (1858-1940). American Jewish lawyer, community leader and vice-president of the American Jewish Congress.
[136] (1872-1937). American Jewish author, journalist, Zionist leader born in London, who was the American Jewish Congress delegate to the Versailles Peace

Conference, 1919.

[137] (1876-1963). United States Zionist leader, journalist, author, co-founder of the American Jewish Congress.

[138] (1856-1946). American jurist and first Jew to sit on the U.S. Supreme Court.

[139] (1867-1928). Union organizer in the clothing industry in New York. Active in the Zionist Movement and a founder of the American Jewish Congress. Member of the Jewish delegation to the Versailles Peace Conference, 1919.

[140] Abraham Goldberg (1883-1942). American Zionist leader and journalist. Co-founder of the Poalei Zion in the United States.

[141] (1867-1924). Zionist leader and author. Born in Byelorussia, settled in New York in 1907 where he contributed to Yiddish journals. Theoretician of socialist Zionism. A founder of the American Jewish Congress and delegate to the Versailles Peace Conference in 1919. See "Yiddishism and Hebraism," page 137.

[142] (1865-1943). Philosopher and essayist. Born in Russia where he was active as a socialist and Jewish nationalist. Elected to the first Duma but could not take his seat because of his revolutionary past. In 1908 settled in New York and became active as a writer and speaker advocating Jewish nationalism, socialism and Yiddishism. See page 137.

[143] (1869-1933). Born in Latvia, he went to the U.S. in 1887 where he played a leading role in the American Socialist Party which was founded in 1900. He learned Yiddish in order to participate in the Jewish trade union movement.

[144] (1871-1926). Lawyer and union activist who emigrated to New York in 1891, member of the Socialist Party of America and elected to the U.S. Congress in 1914, 1916, and 1920 as a socialist.

[145] Benjamin Schlesinger (1876-1932). American trade union leader and managing editor of the *Forward* from 1907 to 1914. President of the International Ladies' Garment Workers Union (ILGWU) between 1914 and 1923.

[146] Abraham Isaac Shiplacoff (1877-1943). U.S. labour leader who organized the tailors' general strike 1920-21. First Socialist elected to New York State Assembly 1915-18. President of the International Leather Goods Workers Union 1927-30.

[147] (1866-1928). One of the founders of the *Forward* in 1897 and a leader of New York tailors' strike of 1912.

[148] (1863-1926). An Egyptologist who became a literary critic and, under pseudonyms, a writer of popular novels.

[149] The *Yidishe Tageblatt*, the first Yiddish daily founded in 1885 in New York, was conservative, traditional, and against socialism and atheism.

[150] (1851-1922). Emigrated to New York in 1886 where he wrote plays and operettas, and is said to have written sixty-four novels which were serialized in the *Tageblatt*.

[151] Most common pseudonym of Israel Joseph Zevin (1872-1926). Born in Byelorussia, he was a pioneer of the Yiddish press in America.

[152] A weekly anarchist paper founded in 1889 which later became the longest lasting weekly Yiddish paper in America, the *Freie Arbeiter Shtime*.

[153] A Hebrew word, literally "taking off," referring to a ceremony performed to relieve a man of the obligation to marry his brother's childless widow. Without the *khalitse,* the widow is forbidden to marry anyone else.

[154] See note 56.

[155] Abraham Cahan (1860-1951). A socialist and orator, he came to the U.S. from Lithuania in 1882. He organized the first Jewish tailor's union. Editor of the *Jewish Daily Forward* from its inception in 1897, he was also known for his novel in English about the urban immigrant experience, *The Rise of David Levinsky.*

[156] See note 49.

[157] "Many readers will recall that during their first few years here they would often pay a visit to Ram's Steamship Ticket Office on St. Dominique Street, near the Labour Temple, to pay for their tickets or to send money to their families in Europe...In addition to Ram's Ticket Agency, there was another popular one – that of Holstein & Haskel. Many readers will perhaps recall that after coming here, on a ticket bought through Holstein's office, for the first few years they also lived in one of his houses on Notre Dame Street West." *Canadian Jewish Chronicle,* March 13, 1936, "Glimpses of the Immigrant's Struggle" by I. Medres, translated by Eli Berger.

[158] "Readers will recall that a Yiddish troupe once played in a theatre located on Cadieux Street, corner St. Catherine. Today there is no sign of a theatre. For a short while a Yiddish troupe played at the Royal Theatre on Coté Street, which was for a long time the burlesque theatre of Montreal. At the corner of Prince Arthur and St. Lawrence there now stands a big garage, but a few years ago on that very spot there stood the movie theatre 'Atlantic Palace', and for a while it was a Yiddish theatre where Yiddish melodramas were produced." *The Canadian Jewish Chronicle,* March 13, 1936, "Glimpses of the Immigrant's Struggle" by I. Medres, translated by Eli Berger.

[159] Louis Mitnick (1866-1915). Considered the father of Yiddish theatre in Montreal.

[160] Abraham Goldfaden (1840-1908). Poet, playwright, and composer, he is considered the founder of modern Yiddish theatre. From 1880 his theatre company performed all over the Russian Empire as well as in Paris, London and New York, the city where he spent his last years.

[161] Joseph Lateiner (1853-1935). Playwright whose theatre company had been the chief competitor of Goldfaden's in Odessa. After emigrating to the United States in 1884 he headed one of the two rival Yiddish theatre companies in New York where he wrote and produced about eighty plays.

[162] Jacob Gordin (1853-1909). Born in the Ukraine, he settled in New York in 1891. His plays were a medium for educating the Eastern European Jewish immigrants, and to this end he adapted plays such as King Lear (*Der Yidisher Keynig Lir*) and Goethe's Faust (*Got, mentsh un tayvl*). The Gordin era is referred to as the Golden Age of Yiddish Theatre.

[163] See chapter on the *Keneder Adler,* page 74 and note 94.

[164] Peretz Hirshbein (1880-1948).Yiddish playwright, producer, and director who from 1911 lived in the United States. His play *Grine Felder* was later made into a movie.
[165] See note 49.
[166] See chapter on the first Jewish bookstore and note 52.
[167] See chapter on the *Keneder Adler*, page 74 and note 94.
[168] (1855-1926). Born in Odessa, he settled in New York in 1890 where he became the star of the Yiddish stage and a leading director and producer of Yiddish theatre.
[169] (1858-1914). Extremely popular and gifted comedian, singer, and dancer in Adler's theatre company.
[170] (1860-1920). Leading actor and theatre manager. He established the David Kessler Theatre in 1913.
[171] (1866-1939). Singer, actor and producer of Yiddish theatre.
[172] (1856-1918). Born in Zhitomir to orthodox Jews, she ran away to join Goldfaden's theatre company and was brought to New York by Adler. She is reputed to have performed the role of *Mirele Efros* by Jacob Gordin 1,500 times.
[173] (1874-1949).
[174] (1875-1939). Once the leading lady in the Imperial Theatre in Bucharest, she arrived in New York in 1895 where she began to appear in the Yiddish theatre. She has been called the prettiest woman on the New York Yiddish stage, and became the first actress from the Yiddish theatre to appear on the English stage.
[175] This play was an example of how its author, Jacob Gordin, used melodrama to educate his audiences.
[176] Isidore Zolatorevsky (born 1873), author of numerous plays for the Yiddish theatre, wrote the play *The White Slave* which was a great success in New York during the 1908-09 season. It was published in book form in 1910, and an English version also appeared. From 1911 until the 1920s it was continuously performed in Europe. In a review in the *Keneder Adler* on May 30, 1910, I. Yampolsky called *The White Slave* "a production on prostitution which had less than no merit." Mme Liptzen played the title role 125 times before appearing in Montreal in 1910. It was Zolatorevsky who brought Louis Mitnick and his theatre company to Montreal in 1896 where Zolatorevsky was living at the time. Thus Zolatorevsky has been credited with bringing Yiddish theatre to Montreal.
[177] See page 89, "Boarders."
[178] (1882-1925). Pseudonym of Katriel Shub. Journalist, lecturer, Yiddishist and Labour Zionist and one of the important speakers at the Chernovitz Conference in 1908 where Yiddish was declared a national language of the Jews. He lived in Montreal in 1911-12, although he had been contributing to the *Keneder Adler* since 1908. See page 144, On the Eve of the Storm.
[179] Louis M. Benjamin (1887-1964). Born in Rumania, he came to Montreal as a young man. A lawyer, he obtained a Ph.D. from McGill University after having studied philosophy and literature at the Sorbonne. From 1911 he wrote articles, poems, and stories for the *Keneder Adler* and other Yiddish publications in Canada

as well as the English-language press.

[180] Hannaniah Meir Caiserman (1884-1950). Born in Rumania, he emigrated to Montreal in 1910 where he was active in the Jewish trade union movement and the Labour Zionists. He helped found the Canadian Jewish Congress (1917-19) and various other Jewish institutions. See "The Canadian Jewish Congress," page 166.

[181] Baruch Goldstein (1879-1953) Playwright, novelist, translator and journalist who was one of the early writers for the *Keneder Adler* during his brief stay in Montreal. In 1920 he moved to New York where he became a theatre critic and director.

[182] (1886-1976). Lexicographer and journalist, born in the Ukraine. From 1913 to 1917 he lived in Montreal where he was active in the Labour Zionist movement and Jewish community activities. He later settled in Israel, achieving prominence as a scholar.

[183] (1894-1964). Musicologist, writer, and editor. He lived in Montreal from 1911, and from 1924 to 1964 he was the editor-in-chief of the *Keneder Adler*.

[184] (1888-1960). As producer, director and actor he was one of the most important figures in the American Yiddish theatre in New York. In 1918 he founded the Yiddish Art Theatre in New York, producing over 150 plays by famous Jewish playwrights as well as world classics in translation.

[185] Born in Minsk in 1890, he travelled throughout Eastern Europe on the Yiddish stage before going to New York in 1912 where he appeared in both Yiddish and English-language plays. He was a co-founder of the Yiddish Art Theatre.

[186] The Fairyland on Notre Dame Street, near Inspector, was the movie theatre frequented by the immigrants. I. Medres, *Canadian Jewish Chronicle*, February 21, 1936, page 5

[187] Words by Anschel Schorr (1871-1942), music by Arnold Perlmutter (1859-1953) and Herman Wohl (1877-1936), this song was written in 1908 in the U.S. and became popular even in Eastern Europe.

[188] *Yisrolik, kum aheym*: words by Louis Gilrod (1867-1930), music by David Meyerowitz (1867-1943). Often erroneously attributed to Goldfaden.

[189] A song about the boatmen on the Volga River, the words are virtually untranslatable.

[190] Text and music by S. Shmulewitz (1868-1943). Popular in Europe as well as in North America during the immigrant era.

[191] Words by Louis Gilrod (1879-1930), music by David Meyerowitz (1867-1943), the song was written for Z. Libin's play *Di gebrokhene hertser* (The Broken Hearts), 1903, where it was sung by the actor Jacob P. Adler and later performed in every Yiddish theatre in the world. In the ghetto the song assumed a negative meaning. Eleanor Gordon Mlotek and Joseph Mlotek, *Pearls of Yiddish Song*, New York: Education Department of the Workmen's Circle, 1988.

[192] Again, the theme of the white slave.

[193] *Yisrolik, kum aheym*. See note 188 above. *Es shaynt di levone*: words by Simon S. Frug (1860-1916).

[194] See notes 43, 96, 97.

[195] (1844-1910). Confirmed as mayor of Vienna in 1897 by Franz Josef I, his administration discriminated against Jews.

[196] David Wolffsohn (1856-1914). Timber merchant, Zionist leader, he succeeded Herzl as president of the World Zionist movement in 1905, a position he held until 1911.

[197] See note 17.

[198] See note 72.

[199] See note 74.

[200] (1867-1935) Hebrew and Yiddish writer, rabbi, and Zionist leader, he represented Vilna in the first Russian State Duma of 1906 and later settled in Palestine.

[201] Menahem Mendl Ussishkin (1863-1941) Born in Russia, he was an early supporter of Herzl who advocated "synthetic Zionism" fusing political activity with practical work in Palestine where he settled in 1919 to become one of the leading figures in the Jewish community.

[202] Clarence de Sola's father, Abraham de Sola (1825-1882), came from a rabbinical family in London, England. Arriving in Montreal in 1847, he became a lecturer in Hebrew and rabbinical literature at McGill University and participated in numismatic and scientific societies. In addition to his position as a leading scholar in the non-Jewish world, he became the rabbi of the Shearith Israel Congregation, the Spanish and Portuguese Synagogue, to be succeeded by son, Meldola de Sola.

[203] See chapter on the Jewish Press.

[204] (1812-1875). Born in Germany, but active in France, he was a precursor of modern Zionism, especially Zionist socialism.

[205] Rome and Jerusalem, 1862, was rediscovered with the birth of the Zionist movement and became a classic of Zionist literature.

[206] See chapter on the Press.

[207] Ferdinand Lassalle (1835-1864) German Jewish lawyer and socialist leader who was a founder of Germany's first workers' party.

[208] See "Zionist Politics," page 110ff., and note 20.

[209] See "Religious Observance," page 34ff.; "The Attack on the Talmud," page 24ff., and note 29.

[210] See "Baron de Hirsh Institute," page 26ff., and and note 22.

[211] Rabbi Nathan Gordon, born in New Orleans, served as rabbi of Temple Emanu-El from 1906 to 1911 after which he became a lawyer and chief counsel of the Amalgamated Clothing Workers. He was also an instructor in oriental languages at McGill University.

[212] Joseph Samuel Leo, born in London in 1859, arrived in Montreal in 1883 and established the first wholesale optical company in Canada, National Optical, in 1912. He was active in Zionist organizations.

[213] See note 23.

[214] Area from Notre Dame Street to the Canal and from McCord to McGill Street.

Many businesses connected with the junk and rag trade were located there.
[215] Russian term for village policemen
[216] The Gunzburgs were a Russian Jewish family of bankers and philanthropists. Baron Joseph Yozel Gunzburg (1812-1878) founded the Society for the Promotion of Culture among the Jews and was made a baron in 1874 by the Grand Duke of Hesse-Darmstadt. His son Horace (1833-1908), continuing his father's activities, became one of the principal spokesmen for the Jews of Russia. His son, Baron David Gunzburg (1857-1910), a scholar and editor-in-chief of the Russian *Jewish Encyclopedia*, was also a leader of the Jewish Community in Russia.
[217] See note 37.
[218] See notes 105, 106, 107.
[219] Born in New York in 1861, he was a prominent clothing manufacturer who was elected to represent the St. Louis Ward and served three terms on the Montreal City Council.
[220] Born in Montreal in 1879, in 1911 he became the youngest barrister in Canada to be appointed King's Council. In 1916 he was elected to the Quebec Legislature as a Liberal from the St. Louis Ward. As a lawyer, he was known as a champion of the poor, the underprivileged, and the workers. See "Attack on the Talmud," page 124.
[221] Samuel William Jacobs (1871-1938). Prominent lawyer, president of the Baron de Hirsch Institute from 1912 to 1914, elected to the Parliament of Canada for the St. Louis Ward in 1917. See "Attack on the Talmud," page 124.
[222] As above and note 221.
[223] See note 220.
[224] 1889-1956 See chapter on the Attack on the Talmud. Born in Austria in 1889, educated in Montreal and Quebec City, he was one of the founders and organizers of the Zionist Organization of Canada of which he was vice-president. A brilliant lawyer, he was influential in the Conservative Party and eventually was elected to the Quebec Legislature as a representative of the Union Nationale.
[225] Marcus Meyer Sperber was a lawyer and editor of the *Jewish Times*. He was also active in many Jewish organizations including the Baron de Hirsch Institute, the Talmud Torah, and the Jewish Immigrant Aid Society.
[226] Joseph-Guillaume-Arthur D'Amours, born in Trois Pistoles in 1865 and ordained in Rome in 1898, lived in St.Roch parish at the time of the Plamondon affair.
[227] As a partner of Lawrence A. Cannon, Taschereau, soon to be Liberal premier of Quebec from 1920 to 1936, was closely associated with this case.
[228] Jean-Thomas Nadeau, teacher of Greek and history, was on the staff of the *Semaine religieuse*, the semi-official organ of the diocese of Quebec.
[229] Joseph-Emery Grandbois. Ordained as a priest in 1896, he had studied at the Dominican School of Biblical Studies in Jerusalem and taught theology at the Grand séminaire de Québec.
[230] (1861-1944). Outstanding church figure in Canada and father of F.R. Scott, humanitarian, lawyer, and poet.

[231] Abbé Maximilien de Lamarque who translated and revised *Der Talmud Jude* by Auguste Rohling and published it in 1888 in Belgium under the title *Le juif talmudiste*. Plamondon relied heavily on this book for information on the Talmud.
[232] Menahem Mendel Beilis (1874-1934). Victim of a blood libel charge in Kiev in 1911, he was accused of murdering a twelve-year-old boy and imprisoned for two years before being tried and acquitted in 1913. The case drew international attention and provoked protests by Jews and liberals.
[233] Ezekiel Hart (1870-1843), a merchant from Trois Rivières, was first elected to the Legislative Assembly of Lower Canada in 1807, but not allowed to take his seat because his oath of office on the Hebrew Bible was challenged. Again elected in 1808, the sincerity of his oath of office, this time on the New Testament, was again challenged. In 1832 "An Act to Declare Persons Professing the Jewish Religion Entitled to all the Rights and Privileges of the other Subjects of His Majesty in this Province" was given royal assent. Hart ultimately took his oath of office on the Old Testament wearing a hat.
[234] See "Hebraists," page 64 and note 68.
[235] On Guy Street south of de Maisonneuve.
[236] Wolf Chaitman was a tailor and union leader who began as a volunteer teacher and remained a teacher at the Peretz School until his old age.
[237] See "Art and Business," page 98 and note 182.
[238] Author of Yiddish books who had attended graduate school at Columbia University, in Montreal he received his M.A. from McGill and became the principal of the Jewish People's School in 1913.
[239] See chapter on the Press for these names. Prof. Hourwich was an economist, writer, and English-language spokesman for the Jews of New York at this time.
[240] See "Art and Business," page 97 and note 182.
[241] (1884-1963). Journalist and scholar who with Ber Borochov founded the Poalei Zion Party in the Ukraine, and eventually became the second president of the State of Israel.
[242] Lord Lionel Walter Rothschild (1868-1937). Zionist and recipient of the Balfour Declaration, 1917.
[243] Edwin Samuel Montagu (1869-1927). Second Lord Swaythling, of an English Jewish family of bankers and philanthropists. His opposition to Zionism led to changes in the Balfour Declaration.
[244] See "Zionist War Policy," page 159.
[245] (1856-1943). A preacher in Russia, he settled in New York in 1895 where he was a popular Yiddish speaker, active in Zionist and religious circles.
[246] Today Dnepropetrovsk.
[247] See "The Historic Zionist Conference," page 115.
[248] Organization founded in the U.S. in 1924, and run by Jewish communists, to promote Jewish colonization in the Soviet Union. After concentrating its efforts on Birobidjan, it disappeared before the end of World War II.
[249] Organization founded in 1924 by the American Joint Distribution Committee

to resettle on the land Jews who had been eliminated from their trades and businesses by the Soviet government. Between 1924 and 1938 it spent nearly $16 million to resettle a quarter of a million Jews in colonies in the Crimea and the Ukraine.

[250] Vladimir Jabotinsky (1880-1940). Born in Odessa, from 1903 he campaigned for Jewish self-defence, minority and civic rights, and the revival of Hebrew. In 1920 he was arrested by the British authorities for organizing Jewish self-defence in Jerusalem. In 1925 he founded the Zionist Revisionists in opposition to official Zionism.

[251] Edmond James, Baron de Rothschild (1845-1943). Philanthropist from the French branch of the Rothschilds, and from 1883 a supporter of Jewish settlements in Palestine.

[252] Today the United Jewish Appeal.

Glossary

TRANSLATOR'S NOTE

In general I have tried to transliterate Yiddish words according to the standard system devised by the YIVO Institute for Jewish Research. However, for commonly used words and names such as Hasidism, 'Chaim' Zhitlovsky, I have retained the spelling in customary usage, rather than the unfamiliar *Khasidizm* or *Khayim*. Where the Hebrew pronunciation of certain words is in common use, I transliterated these words accordingly.

aliyah: call to read a portion of the Torah in the synagogue, considered an honour.

Alphonse: pimp, procurer

Bar Mitzvah: ceremony of admission of a boy at the age of thirteen to the adult Jewish community. Strictly speaking, the term applies to the boy himself.

bima: platform or podium in a synagogue from which the Torah is read.

Bund (Jewish Labour Bund abbreviated from the "General Jewish Workers' Union in Lithuania, Poland, and Russia"): Jewish socialist party founded in Vilna in 1897 committed to Yiddish and secular Jewish nationalism, while opposed to Zionism.

Chanukah: eight-day holiday commemorating the rededication of the Temple in Jerusalem by the Maccabees, observed by lighting the menorah.

Chibat Zion: Literally, Love of Zion. A mid-19th century movement advocating the "normalization" of Jewish life through a return to the ancestral Land of Israel.

Chumash: the Pentateuch (the first five books of the Bible).

Eretz Israel or Land of Israel: name used by the Jews for Palestine prior the establishment of the State of Israel.

eydem af kest: a son-in-law supported financially by his father-in-law.

Eyn Ya'akov: literally, "the spring of Jacob", the title of a popular religious book from the 16th century containing legends from the Talmud by Rabbi Ya'akov, son of Shlomo Ibn Haviv.

fusgeyers: walker, wayfarers.

gabai: manager of a synagogue.

Gemara: the part of the Talmud that comments on the Mishna.

Haftarah: a chapter from the Prophets read in the synagogue following the reading from the Torah.

Haggadah: book containing the story of the exodus from Egypt, read on Passover.

Hasidism: A movement of Jewish religious revival which began in Eastern Europe in the latter part of the 18th century, characterized by pious devotion and joyful worship. Devotees are called Hasidim, the singular is Hasid, and the adjective is Hasidic.

Haskalah: movement for Jewish enlightenment which arose in Germany and Eastern Europe in the 18th and 19th centuries.

kaddish: a prayer said by a mourner.

keneynehore: "May the evil eye be averted."

khalitse: ceremony performed to relieve a man of the obligation to marry his brother's childless widow. Without the *khalitse,* the widow is forbidden to re-marry.

Khok le Yisroel: a book containing extracts from the Bible, the Talmud and other holy books, divided into sections to be read every day of the week.

khside-umes-ho'oylem: gentile friends of the Jews

khupah: canopy under which the marriage ceremony takes place.

khurbn: destruction, catastrophe.

kine: a poem lamenting the destruction of Jerusalem or other catastrophes in Jewish history.

klapper: someone employed by a peddler to sell door to door.

kneydlakh: "matzoh balls," dumplings made of matzoh, the unleavened bread eaten during Passover.

kosher: clean or fit to eat in conformity with Jewish dietary laws.

landsman, pl. *landslayt*: a Jew who comes from the same town in the old country.

landsmanshaft: society of immigrant Jews from the same town or region in the old country.

Litvak: Jew who came from *Lite* (Jewish Lithuania) which included Lithuania, Latvia and Byelorussia.

magid pl .*magidim*: itinerant preacher.

maskil, pl. *maskilim*: adherent of the Haskalah, the movement for Jewish enlightenment.

melamed, pl. *melamdim*: teacher of children.

menorah: eight-branched candelabrum used at Chanukah.

Mishna: collection of post-Biblical laws and rabbinical interpretations compiled around 200 C.E., which forms the basis of the Talmud.

mishnayes: the six volumes of the *Mishna.*

misnagdim: observant Jews who are opponents of Hasidism.

ornkoydesh: ark in a synagogue containing the scrolls of the Torah.

oyhev-yisroel: friend of the Jewish people

Passover: holiday commemorating the Jewish exodus from Egypt.

pilpul: hair-splitting argumentation; Talmudic casuistry.

Poalei Zion: Labour Zionist movement which has as its aim the creation of a Jewish society in Eretz Israel based on socialism.

Polack: Jew from Poland.

Purim: festival commemorating the deliverance of the Jews of the Persian Empire.

Rosh Hashana: Jewish New Year.

seder: festive Passover meal at which the story of the exodus is narrated.

shadkhn, pl.*shadkhonim*: matchmaker.

shir-hamales, pl. *shir-hamalesn*: literally "psalms of ascent," Book of Psalms chapters 120 to 142. Amulet in the form of a leaflet containing the text of Psalm 121 as well as prescribed Hebrew words and phrases. The leaflets are posted on the four walls of a birthing room to ward off evil spirits, in particular the demon Lilith. Also called in Yiddish a *kimpetbriv.*

shoikhet, pl. *shokhtim*: ritual slaughterer.

shtetl: a Jewish town in Eastern Europe.

shul: synagogue.

shund: trash, used in reference to the inferior melodramas of the Yiddish theatre.

siddur: daily prayer book.

Sukkoth: Feast of Tabernacles.

talles, pl. *taleysim*: shawl worn by Jewish men during morning prayers.

Talmud: collection of writings constituting Jewish civil and religious law. It consists of two parts, the Mishna (text) and the Gemara (commentary).

Talmud Torah: religious school for Jewish boys.

tefillin: phylacteries, consisting of two small boxes, with leather straps attached, enclosing Biblical texts inscribed on parchment worn during weekday morning prayers.

Torah: the first five books of the Bible. The term may also refer to the scrolls read in the synagogue, and, in its broader meaning, to all Jewish law and learning.

treyf: food forbidden by Jewish dietary law; used colloquially to mean something forbidden.

tsitses: fringed undergarment worn by observant Jewish males. More accurately, the term refers to the fringes themselves.

uryadnik: Russian village policeman.

yeshiva: institution of higher Jewish learning.

Yom Kippur: one of the Jewish High Holidays, the Day of Atonement, the most solemn fast day in the Jewish calendar.

Selected Bibliography

Abella, Irving, *A Coat of Many Colours,* Toronto: Lester & Orpen Dennys Limited, 1990.

Abramson, Glenda, ed.; advisory editors Dovid Katz et al., *The Blackwell Companion to Jewish Culture,* Oxford: Basil Blackwell, Inc., 1989.

Belkin, Simon. Le mouvement ouvrier juif au Canada 1904-1920, Sillery, Quebec: Les Éditions du Septentrion, 1999.

Berger, David, ed., *The Legacy of Jewish Migration: 1881 and its Impact*, New York: Columbia University Press, 1983.

Brown, Michael, *Jew or Juif? Jews, French Canadians, and Anglo-Canadians, 1759-1914*, Philadelphia: Jewish Publication Society, 1987).

Dobroszycki, Lucjan and Barbara Kirshenblatt-Gimblett, *Image Before My Eyes: A Photographic History of Jewish Life in Poland 1864-1936*, New York: Shocken Books Inc., 1977.

Dubnow, S.M., *History of the Jews in Russia and Poland*, volume 3, Philadelphia: Jewish Publication Society of America, 1920.

Fishman, J., ed., *Studies in Modern Jewish Social History*, New York: Ktav Publishing House, Inc., 1972.

Fox, Chaim Leib, *100 Years of Yiddish and Hebrew Literature in Canada* [Yiddish], Montreal: Adler Printing Reg., 1980.

Frumkin, J.G., ed., *Russian Jewry, 1860-1917*, New York: T. Yoseloff, 1966.

Gitelman, Zvi, *A Century of Ambivalence: The Jews of Russia and the Soviet Union, 1881 to the Present*, New York: YIVO Institute for Jewish Research, 1988.

Greenberg, L., *The Jews in Russia*, volume II, New Haven: Yale University Press, 1965.

Hapgood, Hutchins, *The Spirit of the Ghetto (Studies of the Jewish Quarter of New York)*, New York: Schocken Books Inc., 1976.

Harshav, Benjamin, *Language in Time of Revolution*, Berkeley: University of California Press, 1993.

Hart, Arthur Daniel, *The Jew in Canada,* Toronto and Montreal: Jewish Publications Limited, 1926.

Howe, Irving and Kenneth Libo, *How We Lived, 1880-1930,* New York: Richard Marek Publishers, 1979.

Howe, Irving, *World of Our Fathers,* New York: Harcourt Brace Jovanovich, 1976.

Liptzin, Sol, *A History of Yiddish Literature*, New York: Jonathan David Publishers, Inc., 1972.

Mendelsohn, E., *Class Struggle in the Pale*, Cambridge: Cambridge University Press, 1970.

Mlotek, Eleanor Gordon and Joseph Mlotek, *Pearls of Yiddish Song*, New York: Workmen's Circle Education Department, 1988.

Robinson, Ira, et al. *An Everyday Miracle: Yiddish Culture in Montreal,* Montreal: Véhicule Press, 1990.

Rome, David, *Canadian Jewish Archives*, New Series, Montreal: Canadian Jewish Congress, 1974-96. Almost all of the forty-eight volumes in this series contain detailed information about the Jews of Montreal up to World War I.

Rosenberg, Louis, *Canada's Jews, A Social and Economic Study of the Jews in Canada in the 1930s,* Montreal: Bureau of Social and Economic research, Canadian Jewish Congress, 1939.

Tulchinsky, Gerald, *Taking Root: The Origins of the Canadian Jewish Community,* Toronto: Lester Publishing Limited, 1992.

Zylbercwaig, Zalmen, *Lexicon of the Yiddish Theatre* [Yiddish], New York: The Hebrew Actors Union of America, 1931.

Index

Aberdeen School 81, 135
Abramowitz, Dr. H. 116, 127, 130, 135-36, 157
Amalgamated Clothing Workers of America 142
Agro-Joint (American Jewish Joint Agricultural Corporation 171
Anarchists and anarchism 46, 50-54, 62, 112
Anctil, Pierre 19
Ansell, David 30
Anti-Semitism: Canada 168; Poland 177; Quebec 118, 121-136; Queen's University (Kingston) 143; Russia 16, 73, 160
Arbeiter Ring 45-47, 81
Aronson, Michael 84
Ashkenazim 15
Assimilation 38, 174
Association of Polish Jews 171
Association of Ukrainian Jews 171
Austria 15, 37

B'nai Jacob Synaogue 22, 38-39
Balfour Declaration 154, 160-61, 172
Balfour, Lord 160
Baron de Hirsch Institute 24, 26-30, 65, 150, 152, 168, 177
Barsky, H. 169-170
Beilis case 133
Belkin, S. 151, 167, 174
Ben-Gurion, David 18, 155
Benjamin, Louis M. 98

Ben-Zvi, Yitzhak 18, 154
Bercovitch, Peter 123, 143
Bernstein, Chaim 111
Bessarabia: pogroms 73
Bessarabian Hebrew Sick Benefit Society 81
Beth David Synagogue 22, 38
Beutel, Ben 165
Beys Yosef ve Shmeul Synagogue 165
Bialik School 165
Bialystok 16-17
Blumenthal, Abraham 120, 143
Boarders 89-91
Bolshevik Revolution 158
Booksellers and bookselling 56-66, 82, 141, 165
Bourassa, Henri 122-23
Brainin, Reuben 66, 98, 126, 129, 144-45, 152, 157, 167
Brandeis, Louis D. 159
British army 154. See also Jewish Legion
Bronfman, Abe 165
Bronfman, Alan 143
Bronfman, Samuel 168
Bund 16, 45
Byelorussia 18; pogroms 73; Yiddish in 15

Caiserman, H.M. 98, 141, 144, 151, 168-70, 174, 177
Canadian army 154, 178; Jewish enlistment 152-53; Jewish

regiment 152
Canadian Jewish Alliance 156-57
Canadian Jewish Congress 166-68,
170, 172
Canadian Pacific Railway (CPR) 25,
35, 162
Canadian Relief Committee 157
Cannon, Lawrence A. 125-26, 130
Chaitman, Wolf 138
Chazanovitch, Leon 98, 144
Chevra Kadisha Synagogue 22
Chevra Shaas Synagogue 22
Chibat Zion 73, 188
Citizens League 80, 118-20
Cloakmakers Union 139-40, 176
Cohen, Lazarus 30
Cohen, Lyon 30, 116, 167-68, 170,
172, 175
Cohen, Rabbi Zvi 116, 129, 152,
157, 167, 169-70, 177
Coviensky, L. 177
Creelman, Col. 167

D'Amours, Abbé 127-28, 130
Darwin, R. 111
Davis, Sir Mortimer B. 175
De Haas, Jacob 159
De Sola, Clarence 30, 110-11, 116,
160-61, 167
Depression (1907-08) 67-69, 81
Depression , The Great (1929) 14
Dickstein, M. 138
Dominion Park 106
Drumont, Edouard 122
Dubnow, Simon 16
Dufferin Park 21-22, 36, 67, 70
Dufferin School 21-22, 81

Education: learning English 28-29;

night school 27-28; religious 165
Eidelberg, Joseph 152
Elstein's bookstore 141
Ezra bookstore 66

Farming settlements (Canada) 29-30
Fineberg, Z. 43
Fitch, Louis 111, 123, 125, 130,
169-70, 172, 177
Fletcher's Field 172
Folksfarband 156-57
Folkszeitung 98, 144
Forverts. See Forward
Forward 46-47, 51, 56, 58, 87-88, 90,
94, 112
Fraser's Hall 117
Freedman, Isidore 152
Freie Arbeiter Shtime (Voice of the Free
Worker) 46, 53
Freiman, A.J. 161
Freiman, Lillian 161, 178
Friedman Company 142

Gallay, Joseph 19
Gayety Theatre 159
General Workers' Union. See Bund
Germany 37, 156, 160, 168; Holo-
caust 158, 179
Gold, Isaac 165
Gold, Shlomo 138
Goldberg, Abraham 159
Goldman, Leon 111
Goldstein, Baruch 98
Goldstein, Maxwell 175
Gordin, Jacob 93, 95
Gordon, Rabbi J. 167-68
Gordon, Rabbi Nathan 116
Grandbois, Abbé Joseph-Emery 127-
128
Greenberg, Eliyahu 151

Griffintown 118

Ha'am, Achad 64, 73, 109
Hadassah 161
Halpern, I. 151
Hamelitz 64
Hart, Ezekiel 132
HaShiloah 64
Hasidim and Hasidism 60, 81-82,
    151, 165, 176
Haskalah (Jewish Enlightenment) 18,
    53, 64, 73
Hatsfirah 64
Hayes, Saul 168
Hebraists 64-66, 85, 133, 137-38,
    144, 151
Hebrew Consumptive Aid Society 81
Hebrew Free Loan Association 42-43
Hershman, Hirsch 56, 167, 178
Herzl Dispensary 143
Herzl, Theodore 18
Hirshbein, Israel 171
His Majesty's Theatre 133
Hospitals, Jewish (Montreal) 143
Hovevei Sfat Ever. See Hebraists
Hughes, Sam 152
Hungary 37

ICA. *See* Jewish Colonization
    Association
ICOR 171
Industrial Workers of the World
    (IWW) 140
Intermarriage 38
International Ladies Garment Workers
    Union (ILGWU) 139

Jacobs, Leon V. 169
Jacobs, S.W. 120, 123,125, 129, 143,

150, 152, 167, 169-70
Jewish Agency 155
Jewish Board of Education
    (Montreal) 165
Jewish Colonization Association
    (ICA) 76
Jewish General Hospital 143
Jewish Immigrant Aid Society 177
Jewish Legion 18, 154-55
Jewish People's School (Yidishe folk-
    shule) 138
Jewish Public Library 151
Joseph, Bernard 155

Kach, Shlomo 171
Kahanovitch, Rabbi 167
Kaplansky, Abraham 30, 90
Katzman, S. 151
Kaufman, Dr. Yehuda 98, 138, 151,
    157
Keneder Adler (Canadian Eagle) 13-14,
    17, 19, 28, 66, 73-77, 79-84, 86,
    98, 115-17, 122-23, 126, 129-30,
    141, 145, 149-50; 154, 172, 174
Kishinev: pogrom 73
Kornblitt, Zushe 84
Kruger, Rabbi H. 165

L'Action sociale 125, 128
La Croix 121-22
La Libre Parole 124
Labour Temple 46, 70
Labour Zionists 50-53, 65, 112-15,
    137-38, 144, 154
Landau, Louis. *See* A. Wohliner
Laski, Harold 144
Laurier, Prime Minister Sir Wilfrid
    77-78, 122
Lazarovitch, Louis 126, 131
Le Devoir 123

Leduc, René 125-26, 130, 132-33
Leo, Joseph Samuel 116
Lesser, Charles 152
Levin, A. 111
Levin, Dr. Shmaryahu 159
Liberals 77-78, 82
Lida Yeshiva 18
Liebenson, S. 140
Lithuania 18, 164; Yiddish in 15;
Losinsky, M. 165
Lusitania 160

Magid, M. 165
Malamut, Joel Leib 84
Malbish Arumim Society 81
Margoles, Rabbi Y. M. 165
Marshall, Louis 175
Marxism 56, 113
Masliansky, Rev. Zvi Hirsh 157
McGill University 125, 144
Meighen, Hon. Arthur 159
Mikhlin, M. 138
Miller, Joseph 118
Mizrahi movement 18
Montreal: economic boom 162;
  Port of 31
Monument National Theatre 92-96,
  99, 157-58, 166, 169-70
Mount Royal Arena 172
Mount Sinai Sanitorium 143
Mutual and Sick Benefit Societies 40-
  44, 71, 81
Myerson, Nahum 151

Nadeau, Abbé Jean-Thomas 127-28,
  130
National Radical Schools 18, 137-38
Noveck, H. 138

Odessa 15, 144
Ortenberg, Benjamin 126, 131
Orthodox Jews 34-39, 82

Pale of Settlement 15-16, 18
Palestine 153, 167, 179
Parnes, A. 154
Peace Conference (Versailles) 167-68,
  170
Peretz, I.L. 150
Phillips, Lazarus 117, 165
Plamondon, Joseph Edouard 124-33
Poalei Zion. See Labour Zionists
Pogroms: 16-18, 55, 73, 96, 169-70,
  172
Pointe St. Charles 118
Poland 158, 164, 166, 169, 171, 177;
  12th century 15; 16th century 15
Polish Canadians 171
Poverty 26, 48-49
Prince Arthur Hall 46, 70, 150, 156
Princess Theatre 150
Prussia 15

Queen's University 143

Rabinovitch, Israel 98, 151
Rambach, N. 140
Ravitch, Melekh 19
Recreation 31-32
Reform Jews 36
Reines, Rabbi Jacob 18
Relief committees 156, 174
Religious practice: Bar Mitzvah
  ceremony 34-39; Kashruth 34-35;
  weddings 105-07
Roback, A.A. 84
Rome, David 19
Rothschild, James 175

Rozovich, M. 165
Rubin, Sol 152
Russia 16-17, 164, 170, 172; 18th century 15; alliance against Germany 156; anti-Semitism 16, 147; as an ally 156; elections 17; equal rights 82; Jewish education 146; life under the czar 16-17, 31, 45-56, 73, 147, 152, 157-58; pogroms 16; restrictions on Jews 15, 55; revolution (1905) 17-18, 31, 46, 60; revolution (Bolshevik) 158; unemployment 15; White Guards 172
Russo-Japanese War 18, 31, 55, 73

Sachar, A. 138
Sack, B.G. 84
Sack, Mendel Leib 65, 84
Samuel, Herbert 174
San Remo Conference 172-74
Schiff, Jacob 55, 86
Schubert, Joseph 140
Scott, Reverend F. G. 127-28, 130
Sebag-Montefiore, William 153
Segal, J.I. 9-10, 19, 145
Shaar Hashomayim synagogue 24, 36-39
Shane, Bernard 140
Shearith Israel synagogue 36-37, 111
Shmuelson, Moishe 84
Schneur, M. 144
Shneur, Shlomo 84
Sick Benefit Societies. See Mutual and Sick Benefit Societies
Socialists and socialism 16, 45-47, 50-53, 55-57, 61-63, 86-87, 112-14, 139, 166, 179
Sokolov, Nahum 133-34, 174

Solomon, Alex 152
Spanish and Portuguese synagogue 36-37, 111
Sperber, David 111, 123, 143, 175
St. Helen's Island 31-32, 106
St. Louis Park 135, 165
Steinman, Chaim 118
Stern, Rabbi Dr. H. 36
Steyerman, Benny 118
Strikes and boycotts 70-72, 135-36, 142, 149-50
Sweatshops 67, 95, 164, 176
Synagogues (Montreal) 22, 36-39, 81-82, 92, 165
Syrkin, Dr. Nachman 86, 113, 137

Tageblatt 56, 86
Tailors Union 141-42, 176
Talmud Torah 22, 30-35, 65, 117, 165
Talmudists 85
Tatarinsky, M. 67
Temkin, S. 151
Temple Emanu-El 36

Ukraine 158, 166, 169, 178; pogroms 73; Yiddish in 15
Unions and unionism 29-30, 35, 53-54, 112, 139-142, 144, 149-50

Varheit 86-87
Vaudeville 102-04
Vilna 15, 144, 146
Vilna Gaon 18
Vineberg, Harris 29-30

Warsaw 146
White Guards 172
Wilensky's store 56
Wineberg, Herbert 152

Wise, Rabbi Stephen 36
Wiseman, Shloime 138
Wohliner, A. 84
Wolofsky, H. 74, 135-36, 152, 167,
 170
Workmen's Circle. *See* Arbeiter Ring
Workplace conditions 45, 48-50, 67-
 69, 142
World War I 47, 133, 146-50, 160,
 165; relief committee 156-58
World War II 21, 146, 178
Wortsman, Dr. Ezekiel 84

Yampolsky, Isaac 84
Yiddish, origins of 14-15
Yiddish: education in 137-38; songs
 45-46, 102-04; theatre 92-100;
 use of 40-41; vaudeville 102-04
Yiddishism 137-38

Zeilrei Zion 117
Zhitlovsky, Dr. Chaim 86, 113-14,
 130, 137-38, 167
Zionists and Zionism 18, 30, 36, 45,
 50-51, 65, 83, 86-87, 93-94, 108-
 17, 125, 133-34, 137, 146, 154-
 55, 157, 159-61, 166-68, 172,
 174-75
Zuker, L. 151